THE LAST LEMON GROVE

THE LAST LEMON GROVE

Jackson Webb

Illustrations by Delia Delderfield

WEIDENFELD AND NICOLSON
LONDON

CONTENTS

TO LALLIE AND JAKE
CHARLIE AND MATHEA

Goodbye, my old fan.
Having scribbled on it,
What could I do
But tear it at summer's end?

Basho

INTRODUCTION
Dilys Powell

As you drive west along the coastal road from Chania, the former capital of Crete, you pass just outside the town a monument on a slope to your left. Unexpected in an island not greatly given to public sculpture, it portrays an eagle steeply diving; against the background of trees and modest buildings it looks histrionic. A bus runs past, followed by a car or two. Then the landscape levels. On your right, a tiny bay. The rust-coloured cliffs are not high, but they are steep; a dark shadow suggests a cave. The road runs straight for about ten miles. There are scattered houses. Tall fences of bamboo shelter a nurseryman's ground. The villages have tavernas. One of these has been a mill; the stone arches in the garden where the ducks splash in the water suggest a Venetian origin. The tiny gardens have flowers; beyond them, where on your right the sea sparkles, there is an island; it is a sanctuary of the *agrimi*, the wild horned goat of Crete.

Presently the coastal plain opens to your view. From the low wall which edges the road you look down on a large irregular space, pale green broken by patches of fawn earth. Beyond it, a watercourse, dry now, the banks fraying in the sun; beyond it, the white houses of a village. On the left of the road the ground rises in a gentle slope. Everything is rural, peaceful, the landscape of men and women working with the soil. It is softer, no doubt, than the landscape of *The Last Lemon Grove*; nevertheless one might suppose that it had the same preoccupations.

But the soil here has deathly memories. The rough circle of green pitted with fawn, empty now, quiet on this spring holiday morning, was once the bloody heart of the Battle of Crete: it is Maleme airfield. The shadow of a cave in the rust-coloured bay really is a cave; in 1941 it served as a British field hospital. And the diving eagle? The monument is a German monument. It commemorates the parachutists who three and a half decades ago made their assault on Crete.

Before 1977 I had never seen Maleme. In the years before, I had travelled over a good deal of Crete. I knew, of course, the great palaces, from Phaistos to Zakros. I had watched the windmills on the plain of Lasithi, hundreds of them, fluttering like white blossoms in the breeze. I had gone down the Samaria Gorge, walked a long day's walk over the heights of Mount Ida and climbed to the Idean Cave. Wherever I went I heard stories of the German Occupation. In the lovely Amari Valley people had told me of villages burned and hostages shot. Friends of mine had been killed. I knew the solitary mountain graves of Cretans executed for their part in the Resistance. And I felt that it had all begun with Maleme.

On Maleme and the surrounding area the British hopes had been fixed. It was the scene of the most concentrated attack, the most heroic defence. After Maleme, the desperate retreat over the White Mountains; then the aftermath of defeat, the hunt for fugitives, British, Australian, New Zealand, and the shelter given them by Cretans who risked their own lives. I had almost put the savage passage of history out of my mind. But now, with the spectacle of Maleme airfield I remembered with what emotion we had read the news from Crete in 1941. Life teaches one that no nation is guiltless.

None of us is innocent. All the same I felt a surge of resentment when I thought of the German monument and the diving eagle. From the road it looks like a dive-bomber. It looks like a Stuka.

I had been driven to Maleme by a Cretan friend. Manousos Manousakis cannot have been more than a boy at the time of the war. But like all the best Cretans he was in the Resistance. For the Cretans resisted spontaneously. They came out with any weapons they had; they fought and died as they were, without benefit of uniforms. Manousos recalled clearly the first days of the attack, the planes, the gliders, the deaths. The Cretans, he said, were good marksmen. He remembered one of them taking aim at a German pilot and shooting him precisely in the forehead; he remembered gliders crashing in the watercourse beyond the airfield. Later he knew a German who had a miraculous escape: his glider wrecked, the man found himself on its tail in a shell-hole; he could not believe that he was still alive.

And there were the parachutists. With the directness of a man who has looked battle in the face Manousos described them coming down under fire, hit as they swung: 'You could see them jerk in the air.' Listening, I looked at the airfield and the calm shining sea which had swallowed up so many of the invaders, trapped in their own parachute cords. I looked at the watercourse. It was just like any of the arid streambeds which you find by the score as you walk about Greece. But not to me, not now. I had a vision of the gliders, toppled and splintered, lying between its banks, and their human cargo 'thick bestrewn', like Satan's fallen angels in *Paradise Lost*, 'under amazement of their hideous change'. Out of perhaps a thousand men in one assault wave, Manousos said, less than a hundred were left alive and unhurt. Shattered, they waited for capture. But there was confusion among the Allies. Capture never came.

The Germans, too, made mistakes. They had not counted
on local opposition. On the contrary, they had expected a
friendly and welcoming population. Enraged, General
Student, who commanded the parachute operation, accord-
ing to Manousos ordered the execution of one in twenty of
the available Cretans. Fortunately a wiser and more humane
member of the German staff (he was, Manousos said, to be
among those executed for his share in the 20 July attempt
on Hitler's life) opposed the order and it was never carried
out. Perhaps the German command had not counted, either,
on the cost of the Cretan campaign. For the parachutists it
was almost a massacre; as I listened my resentment dissolved.
I asked Manousos if he still felt bitter about the German
Occupation. No, he said, he was over that. He hadn't forgiven the Italians, but about the Germans he was no longer
bitter.

We drove a few hundred yards inland towards the gentle
incline on the left of the road, and pulled up in the courtyard
of a whitewashed building. Behind it a path wound between
green slopes up the hill. Looking back, one saw the deserted
airfield and the coast curving away to the long promontory
of Cape Spatha. A lorry rattled in the distance; no other
sound except the rustle of leaves and grass and insects which
everywhere in the country is carried on the air. And now
as we climbed the hill we were in a vast, orderly, mathemati-
cal pattern of graves, hundreds of graves, German graves.
And I realized that this was a landscape remote in mood from
the setting of Jackson Webb's book.

The British war cemetery looks over Souda Bay; there,
set in the long lines between slim orange trees, I found the
name of a friend. It is a cemetery much visited by former
combatants. This year a party of Maoris from New Zealand will remember their dead; the British Ambassador in
Athens will be with them. Each cemetery has in its commem-

orative building a book giving the names and their places in the pattern of graves. At Maleme the stone slabs (there are no crosses) with the bright, tidy, punctuating flowers often record unknown victims, often two in one grave. Of the named, nearly all are in their early twenties; few are more than twenty-five years old. It is a place for enormous pity.

And there is a touch of irony. Two Greeks are in charge of the graveyard of the German invaders. Both are Cretans – and not only Cretans. They are famous, they are heroes of the Resistance. Both fought, both may have killed – killed, perhaps, some occupant of a grave on the hillside. Manoli Paterakis – tall, smiling, a long good-tempered nose, a peaked khaki cap – was in the party which, with Paddy Leigh Fermor as leader, kidnapped the German General Kreipe. After the war he went to Germany and paid the General a friendly and welcomed visit. George Psychoundakis – small, thoughtful, a sad face under a leather cap – was another special friend of British liaison officers during the Occupation. He composed an account of his war experiences: *The Cretan Runner*, it was called. It was published in English; the translation was by Leigh Fermor, whose life he is said to have once saved. He is now engaged on translating the Odyssey into modern Greek. I knew that Tom Dunbabin, one of the most distinguished of the liaison officers who served in Crete, would sometimes undertake a mission only if guided by Psychoundakis. Now the Cretan's son, a boy of sixteen, is studying in Germany, where he lives with a German family.

The mood, then, has truly changed. Manousos has forgiven Germany. Manoli pays a friendly visit to his former captive. George Psychoundakis entrusts his son to a German family. During the working week you still hear the roar of bombers over Maleme, but it is the Greek Air Force using the old airfield for target practice. The peace which ruled on the day when I first went there is as permanent as anything can be in the turbulent history of Crete.

In the recent affluence of the north of Crete one can oneself forget the past. The new University of Crete is to be divided between the three major towns, Herakleion, Rethymnon and Chania. Agriculture flourishes and one hears of fresh developments in the production of avocado and banana. From Mallia westward the new hotels go up; tourists aren't bothered by the vagaries of architecture. But obstinately the old Crete survives. Chania, if you take the trouble to look, is full of Venetian memories: great walls, elegant doorways, churches and the noble but neglected shipyards by the harbour. Excavation still brings to light Minoan remains, Roman remains. One restaurant inhabits a tall beamed building, constructed in 1650, with tiered galleries. Walls hung with crimson embroideries, it looks a cross between a splendid Greek manor and the lofty studio of some great seventeenth-century sculptor. One had thought Chania destroyed by war, but the houses and the tavernas on the quayside have the pleasing irregularity of age.

It is a happy city to explore. Nevertheless as I wandered I still could not quite shake off the spell of Maleme. And there was Cape Spatha, that long promontory beyond. A friend who in the war escaped from a German military camp was finally taken off by boat from the headland; he reached Turkey and freedom. I decided to visit Cape Spatha.

From the base of the headland to its point and back would be a long walk, too far for a day, and this was February, with night falling early. It was also the end of Carnival; in Chania boys were running about the quayside in masks. You might, somebody suggested, get a boat from one of the villages on the coast, though amidst the Carnival festivities it wasn't likely. But it was an idea. I got up early next morning and walked by the church of St Nicholas and through narrow streets to the square with the huge cruciform market. A little farther, and I found a bus to Kastelli, which lies at the base of the headland on its west.

There was a restaurant in the square at Kastelli. I ordered a cup of coffee and enquired about boats. The waiter was friendly. But he was not encouraging: no chance of a boat. What about a car, though? No road to the far point of Cape Spatha, but a taxi could take me more than half-way, and there I could see the church of St John Giona. There is a cliff, a gorge, he added vaguely.

A taxi was standing in the square. Reluctantly, for he said the road was very bad, the driver agreed to take me. He hoped we could make it: the road, he said again, was very bad. Back, then, along the main Chania road, half-way round the base of the peninsula; then a turn seawards, climbing through green docile country with ranges of jagged hills on the left. After perhaps three miles a village, Rodhopou. And then indeed a bad road: sharp, grinding, loose stones, huge potholes filled with rainwater, the car swaying and slipping, the driver grumbling. Once, a shepherd with his flock and a barking dog. For ten miles not another living creature; I had the sensation of driving along the spine of the earth. At last – it was noon – we pulled up by a gravelly stretch of pallid grass. There was a wayside shrine. Standing by it, one looked over a precipitous slope into a deep gorge; far away in the depths the tiny church of St John Giona. Yes, said my driver, you go down from here – and there was indeed a winding hairpin path. But it is steep, he went on. It will take you three-quarters of an hour coming up again. And how long to walk back to the main road and a bus? Three hours, he said. And recompensed and thankful he got in his taxi and, grating and roaring over the potholes, he drove home to his lunch.

I am glad now that I went down the path. I hesitated, for had I twisted an ankle on the shifting stones there was nobody to help me – or so I thought until, perhaps an hour later, I reached the church and saw a solitary man working in the fields. One should make the expedition at the end of August, when thousands from Western Crete gather to celebrate the festival of the saint and hang their offerings on the tree in the courtyard. But at any time the landscape is magnificent. In a way, too, I was glad of the solitude. I remembered my friend and his companions tramping the length of that ferocious headland and escaping: a victory, I thought. And here Crete, proud, independent Crete, had asserted itself over the quarrels of humanity. The promontory was untouched, inviolate, as little concerned with war as Jackson Webb's intractable Sfakian countryside. When, panting, I regained the crest of the heights, I was ready to walk cheerfully back to Rodhopou and the main road beyond.

While I waited in the dark for the bus a man who had been gathering firewood asked me if I was German.

'No,' I said, sourly, 'English. Why do you take me for a German?'

'Because German women often travel about the country alone,' he said. Then: 'The English are a truly democratic people, almost the only ones in Western Europe; but England stabbed Greece in the back in the war.'

He was referring to British political intervention in 1944 and 1945; he was, of course, a Communist and owned to it with pride. I tried to refute him. But that open declaration, too, seemed to me to mark a change in the climate of Greece.

Next day the painter John Craxton and I drove from Chania towards the south coast, setting of *The Last Lemon Grove*. On the way we paused to look at a little church hidden in a miniature valley. It had exquisite frescoes; Crete is full of concealed beauties. At the top of the gorge which plunges to Chora Sfakion we stood gazing at the stupendous cliffs

and the sea, dim now in the spring evening. Going back, we
halted in a taverna where John had friends. We drank for
the end of Carnival, drank again with a genial villager who
had turned his house into his own war museum: painted
bomb-noses, guns, Occupation coins and paper money, a
range of cherished and hoarded curiosities, everything gaily
coloured, pennants flying on the verandah. Night among the
Cretan mountains can leave the shadow of fright. I was glad
to be sent home with this lively vision.

For, as we stood looking towards Chora Sfakion and the
sea, I had reflected that somewhere down there, ·vay to the
west, Jackson Webb had lived the solitary days of *The Last
Lemon Grove*. Solitary days: they were shared with the friends
a hermit will adopt – dog and cat, goat and donkey, a visiting
bee, once a hedgehog. Not that he lived apart from the people
around him, country people growing crops often meagre and
struggling every year against the same winds, the same cold,
the same floods. Mr Webb knows those people well. He gave
them what he could and accepted from them their proud
recompense. They advised him as he planted and hoed, they
helped him to build a little house. Few travellers, few Philhel-
lenes have existed in such close touch with the Cretans or
indeed any other Greeks. You might say that Jackson Webb's
life was fused with theirs, that it was the same life. And it
is this illusion of unity with a community alien from our own
experience which gives *The Last Lemon Grove* its unique
quality. I have read no other book quite like it.

And yet despite the proximity with his neighbours Mr
Webb's days were, as I say, solitary. They could not have
been otherwise, for writing is a solitary occupation. Mr
Webb is even a wilful solitary. He once considered with-
drawing to a loneliness even more intense, a discomfort even
sharper than he had so far endured. He thought of moving
on from his Sfakian district to the remote island of Gavdos,

and I have never heard of anybody recommending living on Gavdos.

Nevertheless his instinct for isolation was justified. With whatever sympathy a writer watches, he must still detach himself, still observe from the outside. And it is with a writer's eye that Mr Webb records. The Crete he knows is not the sunny Crete of the pleasure-seeker. It is a harsh land. Reading his book, one would hardly think that it is set in the same island as the soft curves of Maleme. But perhaps that contrast is part of the fascination. For Jackson Webb can write today as if there had been no war, no Occupation. He can look out across the sea and never think of the fearful retreat over the White Mountains and the agonized embarcation from Chora Sfakion for Egypt. He has no concern with the Crete of history, the Crete of battle.

He belongs, really belongs, to the Crete of now.

BURNOOSE

IN THE LATE SUMMER WHEN I RIDE ALONG THE ROAD
to Paleochora, I see the limp little balls of spines tossed
over to the sides of the fields like rocks, or even lying on
the tops of the walls as though on display.

At night, they say, hedgehogs come out and eat the roots
of the crops, and the plants collapse on themselves mysteri-
ously. You can't see anything wrong above the ground, but
the women lift the stalks up by the leaves to show you where
the sharp little teeth have bitten through. The zig-zagging
line of dying okras or cucumbers winds away across the
furrows, and ends.

So the hedgehogs are easily found, dug out and beaten with
short-handled hoes called *tsápas*.

In many ways, Paleochora could be the poorest village on
Crete. The south coast weather is hard, either driving rain
and wind or burning dry heat that opens cracks in the road.
People are lucky to harvest anything at all.

I'm rich, myself: I have half my field for me and the other
half for whatever else might happen. But maybe it's true,
the real damage hedgehogs do to others. I don't know. Only
once were there any of them out near me. I'm always
surprised to see so many killed along the road.

23

One time, I was walking to the end of the river that curves behind these same fields by the road and cuts through the shingle beach to the sea.

It was a soft red and green evening in August, silent, like the end of a year. I felt that something new had come, and I began to look for a change in the stirring grass and each simple stream dwindling back to nothing in the reeds and moss.

There are no rocks in the river there. The water moves by noiselessly, though you can hear it falling just above the mill and washing monotonously onto the coast.

The sun had set behind the peninsula of the town and a new breeze was sighing. The river wound on between the windbreaks of clattering bamboo, with their feathery plumes touching high overhead, twenty or thirty feet from the coils of roots dropping from the stony banks. This was the back fence to the dozen road fields, an impenetrable wall, except to hedgehogs.

I was walking through the lightness of sticks when I saw a prickly fist groping in the wild flowers under a bent plane tree across the water. I'd never seen a live hedgehog before. He seemed a special find, a sign of something. Or else it was just that red evening and all the vague, windy days before that made him seem so.

Like a kind of caterpillar he came to the blowing tree, thought, and then bumbled blindly up it. About a foot off the ground, he paused and turned sideways, balancing stupidly for a moment. Then he fell in the leaves with a faint rustle and lay motionless in a ball.

He heard me splashing over and gave a jerk of his back, arching, so that the mud-matted spines stood on end. And there he sat, headless, almost invisible in the plane burrs that littered the ground.

Was this his protection, then? Just to lie still until I went away? Not much!

24

Yet I found he was almost perfectly resistant when I tried to roll him over with my boot to see his face. He sagged lower on the ground, even put his weight against me – I could feel him pushing and shifting. Each touch sent a fresh rippling through his quills.

So was I merely to look and he merely to wait, and then each of us would go separate ways in the night? Evidently that was all. I tapped him with a bamboo stick and he bristled around it and leaned to repulse that gesture from me. It was infuriating.

'Will you kill him?' I asked myself, bending over.

'No,' I thought, straightening.

I touched him again with the stick, then I quickly turned him over with my hat, expecting to see another half-mound of prickles.

But no! A soft white stomach appeared with four padded feet on it. And two tired, black eyes peered up at me over a long snout, like a fox's, or an old man's.

The helplessness of him! That was what was most surprising, the way he held so still when I might have hurt him.

I poked his hot stomach that moved with slow breaths. Bare and fat, he was. The little face still looked up blankly.

'Shall we take him home?' I asked.

'I don't know,' I said.

'Is he sleeping?'

'I don't know anything about it.'

He seemed unconscious with fright, maybe already dead. I wanted to take my time with him. But when I left him alone, the stomach sank from sight again and the spines turned back up. In an instant those black-button eyes were gone too. And there he lay as before, a Cretan hedgehog.

If I smoothed back the spines, it was easy to lift him up from the leaves, though he sagged one way and the other, trying to fall from my hands.

Someone stopped hoeing in the next field, and a voice called out, 'What do you want?'

So I dropped the hedgehog into my hat and started home along the open beach.

I rolled him onto the oven ledge in the courtyard. With one liquid movement he turned into a ball again.

'Your name is Burnoose.'

I chose the oven as Burnoose's temporary home, until he'd begin to walk about on his own. I pushed him inside, and then I went to the spring to wash my hands. I scythed up some red roots of wild grass from the sides of my field and brought two ears of corn and a cup of water for him. Then I pulled the slate cover across the opening and propped a book against it in the dark.

The next day, I tried to make Burnoose follow me with a crust of bread in my hand. I could see him blinking in there, but not a sound came out, not the slightest movement. Just the whispering sea and the dry weeds stirring in the cracks. What did a hedgehog do? I watched the mud dome of the oven shimmering in the sun.

I asked old Manoli about it, indirectly, because he owns the two long fields and this stone house in the lemon trees.

Manoli smiled because the answer was so easy.

'O-ooh ... o-oooh, it goes.' He scowled up to his cockscomb of white hair and took a grip on his axe. 'When you hear that, you know he's in your field.'

'*Gaff!* ... *Gaff!* it goes,' thought Kristo, Manoli's son, who wears sunglasses and drives a motorcycle-taxi. He leaned unknowingly against the closed oven and tapped the lump of his Luger in his shirt. '*Gaff!* Like a mad dog,' he shrugged without interest. Hedgehogs weren't politics.

Some people told me hedgehogs made no noise at all, that they only ate. Some laughed unkindly and said they had beards, like mine. Others said they made a sniffing, peeping

sound and could run as fast as a mule. Many had never
thought about it.

'Horrible, if he's baking in there,' I stopped and thought
that afternoon, though the flat-roofed house was hotter inside
than the oven without a fire. Maybe it was the loaf-like
appearance of Burnoose before I sealed him in – and now the
silence. There was also the possibility of forgetting about him
altogether.

Evening came. The owl fluttered down to the post outside
my window and the oven dome began to glow like a mosque
in the moonlight. Because of Burnoose, it seemed a lonely
house when I went to sleep that night, not a good place anymore.

Every morning when the sun brightens the carob trees by
the road, my dog Katina stretches and shuffles across the
courtyard into the shady recess under the oven. Then she falls
asleep again in one of her tortured positions on the firewood.

That second morning of Burnoose, she stopped under the grape arbour and bared her teeth with a low growl. Around here, unusual things are bad things. Her brown and white puppy dived into the water ditch, and the black goat Willy side-stepped up the bamboo fence of the lentil field. Morris poked his bowl-cut head around the corner of the house and made his wheezing white-eyed bray. Sofia soared to the kitchen window with one of her kittens in her mouth. I put down my pencil and went to the door.

Katina was circling the oven, barking and coughing. Burnoose had crawled out through the flue and was sitting like a clump of moss on the mud top. At each gnash of teeth, for now Katina was dashing mindlessly at the stone base, Burnoose quivered his quills and settled himself right and left. In a place so poor that hunters shoot sparrows and wasps build their nests in crossings of twigs, this was a fine catch for a dog like Katina.

I quickly righted things. I skidded Burnoose back into his house and plugged the flue with my hat. I scythed some fresh grass for Morris, and after a while Katina snorted and went back to sleep. But it was oddly depressing, the whole, small episode. It seemed as if things were closing on me somehow. More and more often, a little before Burnoose and ever since, I've shown myself to be too brittle and habit-grooved even to bring something new to the house.

It has happened by degrees. I have lived alone in my mind for two years in this corner of the plain between the sea and the first hills. The house *is* lonely. Sometimes in the windy nights I imagine I'm at the end of a great continent or responsibility, or at the finish of a time. The sheep cough, the owl calls, and there are remarkable noises of the darkness that I can't quite put my finger on anymore – water voices, endless singing and sobbing, noises from the trees, noises from the sky. Sofia hears them too. She stops purring and listens with saucer eyes at the foot of the bed. And the daytime is becoming stranger than the night, with all the soldiers and troop trucks going by on the road.

I thought animals would lend a happier, more permanent look to the place. But instead, it's been very tight and intense, because we have to live so close together in this clearing in the lemon grove. Just to get along out here, there must always be a kind of dull compromise among us, predictable, belittling somehow. We're all crammed together, totem-like, watching one another and waiting for separate things. Maybe it's too hard a place? Maybe no one should be living here anymore. Manoli isn't. He's moved into a new concrete house in Paleochora.

Black-bag Sofia suffers most. She hunts for hours in the yellow speargrass between the squares of clover. I see her from my window. She rushes in with her tail flicking, careless and heavy-footed, then she stops still to listen and see if she's frightened anything. This far, it's original and effective. She springs, and tosses up a little lizard or a writhing centipede, trapping it with her paw, hitting it on the head. Then she trots it off down the track to the house with a muffled call, while the hungry sparrows dive and screech. At her unmistakable warning and the tinkle of the goat bell on the door, I have to go in with a broom or a walking stick to oust her cartwheeling brown-and-yellow vipers, flopping bats and scorpions, and, once, an enormous sky-blue land crab that scuttled under the rush mat while Sophia screamed with her eyes closed. Day after day, time after time:

'Oh, no you don't! Let *go*! There! Take it out!'

Willy the goat prefers the kitchen to the outside, since he can't eat my basil and he can't go into the field. The outside offers him nothing.

Katina has learned to sleep from morning to evening. Whatever she does at night is quiet. She is a constant, and constants stabilize things in the summer when the plain is waving meaninglessly in the heat and the sea sparkles out of sight. In the winter when the roof-leaks make muddy streams down the walls and my teeth are chattering like castanets, Katina emerges calmly from under the oven, drinks from the hollows in the courtyard stones and goes back in again. 'Anyway, Katina's holding up to it,' I say, looking out at the splashing rain. And it seems for the moment that this in-turned existence is just tenuous, nothing worse.

I suppose Morris is a constant too. He never does a donkey's work. Except when I ride him into town, he merely walks back and forth to his cave under the cliff. I save the dry piles he makes for the basil.

Johannes the bee also finds living together easier, but humbling. When I'm writing early in the morning, I hear him stirring overhead, picking his way down the hollow bamboo ceiling to the gap at the wall-top. There's a pause and then a rasping, drilling sound, though the scene remains unchanged. Then Johannes steps quietly into the sunshine and the sound begins again. He rises slowly, hovering for a minute, then he drops with a swoop to the knothole in the door and flies into the wind.

He's about as large as a matchbox, coal black, returning each time with a band of orange pollen on both legs. The first time I saw him, I thought he was a bat and that the sound was coming from somewhere else. I put my glasses in my shirt pocket, as my chair spun over backwards and my pencil rolled off the table. Johannes's bright powder sifted uselessly down as each of us fought to get outside.

Gradually our doings have become more or less known to each other. His returns are more startling than his goings-out: a sudden droning from nowhere, and then a silence, with only the carob branches scratching the roof. Then all at once a big black hand fumbles through the knothole and feels around, growing larger and larger. I tell myself: Johannes is coming. But his size is always alarming, especially when only half-seen. A jerk of my hand still makes him pause warily and walk sideways towards the open bamboo, watching to see if our understanding is over.

And there are three salamanders. In the late afternoon when the little sounds of the plain are fading back to town and the shadows of the fence posts stretch longer across the fields, I light the lanterns and there they are again: three salamanders, curled in the far corner of the room as if painted there.

The evening begins with the usual buzzings and pings of bugs against the screens, a quiet time while the holes are found, then many long, looping flights of things to the two lamps hung over the bed. There are polished beetles and tiny jumping spiders, mantises, fireflies, grasshoppers, long-legged mosquitoes and columns of ants suddenly swaying up the walls. And there are moths, inch-worms, cockroaches, earwigs, lady-bugs, and hard-shelled fliers the size of my thumbnail which I call *airplanes* because of their sputtering, lead-like dives into my open hands and coffee cup.

The salamanders lie waiting at odd angles with their black globe eyes blinking approval and their four-toed feet turning them slowly, carefully towards the points of the bugs' long shadows. Then they dash down the wall-cracks at really surprising speeds. It goes on for an hour or more, the rushing and skittering above me, the blurr of movements and wee jaws working vigorously. Pop! Smack! Smack! And still the sombre sound of my pages turning and the hiss of the lamps.

'The little one never moves, does he?' I put down *Emerson's Essays* again. 'No, there he goes with the others.'

The trio gallops to the centre of the ceiling in quick, halting runs, casting their prehistoric shapes as far as the bookshelf. If they get too close to one another, a clicking sound then a low chirping begins, and if one of them meets a snail, there is a small, horrible scream, even louder than the groaning frogs on the windowsill. When I blow the lanterns out, the salamanders are either waiting vacuum-like by the ant-hole over the clothes basket, or slyly by either door for some other night creature I still haven't seen.

Then Burnoose came. We sat on the bench under my window, watching the sun beat down on the oven dome. Katina sleepily snapped at a fly, actually maimed it, and her ears went back with surprise. Johannes jumped on a red poppy, bowing it down to the ground and rasping off its petals until there was only Johannes there. Then it was silent all around the house.

'Poor Burnoose,' I thought.

'The oven door will be left open at night.'

'Yes, and then he'll get away. Or Katina will catch him.'

'She'll be sorry if she does.'

'He'll get away.'

'Not necessarily,' I decided.

That night, I took away the oven door and then went back into the house. An hour later I came out again with my book and glasses and listened for a moment. I felt in all the corners, and finally I crawled inside myself. He was gone.

Evidently, Burnoose had inched to the edge of the oven ledge and down the broken amphora that leans against the wall. In the morning I followed the determined little track down one side of the path to where the grassy water ditch crossed it. I put my hands in my pockets and leaned against a fence post with my scythe stuck in it. Burnoose shouldn't have been called anything.

'Someone here is a crazy man,' Manoli said to me, there being no one else about. 'Hedgehogs are no good. My field, now, my grove, maybe *kaput*.'

'They're all right,' I said.

'Ey, all right! You don't know!' Little Manoli started off with his black knee-boots tramping and his hoe on his shoulder, angry Manoli with his face like a glove and his pointed chin in the air.

Sofia opened the kitchen screen with her head and went to sleep on the table with the flies sparkling around her. The same silence again.

I wondered why I was still here. I drank my coffee and thought of all the prettier, easier places I knew where I could be writing my book – northern places with autumns and butter and better governments, places far away from Crete, back in the sensible wilderness of the past.

'... two of them out there now, bad luck ...' Manoli's voice mumbled from further away.

'Manoli. Two, you said?' I just laughed.

He came back into the courtyard and felt his vest for his box of cigarettes. He offered me one and we sat on the bench.

'Two!' he said. 'Would I lie? They're out there digging holes now. Can't you hear them? They're making holes in my fields. Heard of *holes*?'

'Yes.'

'Eh! Bravo!'

'But, as I told you, I brought only one hedgehog.'

'He brought it, he brought it,' Manoli said.

I knew only Burnoose had come with me from the river that night. But what did that matter, now that Manoli thought he saw two?

'Two, I saw! Two, curse them, from where they went! Maybe more!' Manoli drew two tiresome lines in the dirt with his boot.

It was an important day. For the first time it seemed too hard to live here the way I wanted to, staying calm, seeing small.

'And tomorrow, two,' Manoli opened his hands and leaned forward with a shrug. 'And the next day, my Yakovo, maybe two more ...?'

Hopeless.

YANNI

MANOLI IS IN A RAGE AGAIN, STAMPING HIS FEET IN
the middle of the road, shouting with his hands over his
head. Morris hides in the tall grass, even the birds fly off.

But Yanni's Maria waves him away and bleats right back.
Manoli was watering his trees when she blocked his sluiceway in the grove and flooded her own little plot by the road.
Now the longer the argument goes on, the more water she
helps into her field, scratching with her fingers, kicking at
the last dry clods with her plastic shoes.

'From now on, don't come here!' Manoli calls. 'Tomorrow, don't come! Tomorrow: nothing!'

'Ey, tomorrow!' Maria cackles, tiptoeing through the
mud. 'What was there yesterday? What today?'

Manoli strides into the trees and rolls a boulder into the
winding ditch she's made with a stick. He walks stiffly back
to his lemon saplings staked in rows by the sea. After a minute
the water glimmers down behind him again on the other side
of the road, and the wasps go on buzzing over the mud.

'He's closing us out!' Maria comes and says to me with
her cheek on her shoulder. 'What will our food be now? Eh?
Where will it come from?' She pinches her fingers together
over her mouth.

'Never mind, it'll pass,' I say softly, confidently, the way Yanni does. But it's not enough, and she shakes her head and walks away from my window, mumbling and rubbing her back. She takes her apron off the gatepost, flaps it and starts hopelessly back down the road to town.

Still, Yanni's winter field is ready again this year. In fact, it's ready every year just about this time, though the shouting and trouble are always the same. It's the first day of October, clear and cold, rather like yesterday. At noon, Manoli is sitting on the stone by the spring, as always, and the pale sea still washes in.

The next morning at dawn, Yanni is out cutting his new furrows, throwing his roots and rocks out onto the road. His son Mikalis brings a little trickle of water down behind him, so little that it can almost be a mistake if Manoli comes. He lets each furrow fill to the top, then he frantically rakes it closed with his hands before the tell-tale path to the house is washed over dark.

Then comes Maria, clawing up the dirt and halving the seed potatoes between her knife and her thumb, moving down the rows in a crouch. She starts pushing in broad beans where Yanni's left his red bandana. Next come the tomato plants tied in a bag.

Everyone runs when Yanni starts his winter field. It's a year-long build-up of need and determination, finally as short and sure as the Little Summer of St Dimitrius.

Maria is never late bringing his mushy billy-can lunch of sparrows and snails, and Mikalis rushes everywhere at once in his cauldron trousers and his big burst shoes, calling Ba-baa! and whistling to answer the burst of Yanni's voice. Sometimes there's a long trail of words and then the awful sound of a slap. But usually the work goes on in near-perfect unison. It has to, in this little space of time.

Manoli stops by the oven and clicks his tongue.

'Where are you going?' he calls after whoever runs past him. 'Whose hoe is that? Ey? Mine? And why do you yell like that?'

To Yanni, Manoli says, 'Mr Yanni, if you want to keep this field, don't take the water again while I'm working!'

And he says to me, 'I'm sorry for this, Yakovo, all this noise and difficulty when you're writing. All the little Yannis will be going away from here. Don't worry! This is their last year.'

Yanni pauses, watching from a distance. He lights a cigarette and leans on his hoe.

After four or five days the winter field is done. Mikalis has to water at night only twice more before the rain comes.

Just before Christmas, Maria appears with a basket to carry away her first beans and squash.

Then I don't see much of Yanni, not even in Paleochora. I miss the whistles and shouts and the tramp-tramping outside the house. Often he's borrowed my coat or a little money, but it doesn't matter.

In fact, I don't want him to pay me back any more. It's unpleasant when he comes all the way out here to pay me, both of us knowing he can never return the money completely. But each time, as if the joke is forever new, he reaches slowly into his pocket, smiling and looking sideways, not on his own ground. Not really Yanni at all. Just because of the money.

'Here's one,' he says, putting down a shiny ten drachma piece. 'That buys one hedgehog, right, Yakovo, our clever one, our Wealth? Here's two. . . .' Time and again; it must be blindly gotten through.

'And there's three,' I say, pointing. Uncontrollably my eyes watch his nicked hands coming up with the coins. I wait at the door not because of the money, but because so few people come to see me.

'Three, right – and maybe that's all. Do you think I have more? What do you think?' Yanni stands there proudly without enough money again, hating that, hating me. 'No, no more!' he snorts. 'Finished!' Katina walks away, Morris turns his back and goes on eating, and I'm puzzled and can never say the right thing.

Maybe I shouldn't lend him things. Yet that doesn't seem to be the whole solution. It's hard to get close to Yanni. The moment is never right somehow.

'Don't worry about the old uncle!' Manoli's Kristo says with a laugh. 'Don't worry about Yanni. He comes around when he wants.'

But after a while, even Manoli stops thoughtfully by the

window with his arms folded and his hand axe cocked out behind him. 'That one – very lazy, I say.'

'Who?'

He nods to the little scrap of a field that's bursting with wide green leaves and huge orange squash flowers trailing out onto the road. 'Yanni,' he says. 'He didn't come to help me plough.'

'How many rows did he finally plant himself?'

'I don't know, I didn't see,' Manoli says. 'Listen: once I told him, "Yanni! Come! Take this bit of land of mine, grow what you can there!" He's a poor fellow, Yakovo, devil take it – he has nothing. No clothes, no firewood. You help him and, ey-hey? Now you see what he does with us.'

Many more days pass without Yanni, and soon Manoli's wife Espasia is trotting out all her old stories again: how Maria shut herself up in the house after their wedding forty years ago, and how Yanni had to sleep on the roof and call to her down the chimney. Also, Yanni sold his war medals for a shotgun; cut Espasia's arms off if it's not the truth. Funny, how the Communists left *his* house alone during the trouble. It was a gypsy who put all this bad luck on him in the first place. Didn't Espasia see him hit a gypsy with a stick? And to this day, Maria has never shown anyone her marriage-night sheets.

And other things. I only half-hear. I never knew the difference between an open face and a closed one before I met Manoli's Espasia. Her face is shut tight with suspicion and wrongs, and her bulb nose is a lock on it. Not really shut, but moving away from you somehow, leaving you. You want to stop it with your hands. Its expressions go along with you for a while, especially during a story about Yanni. Then all at once her whole face seems to stop – you can see it congeal around her mouth until only her lips are moving.

Though I suppose Maria's face is really the closed one, wrinkled shut with work, her glance gone as sightless as a cat's.

In any event, the days go by and still no Yanni. Then one clear morning, maybe a Sunday when the church bells are tolling mournfully from Paleochora, and the harsh, closer bells at the cemetery start clanging too, Yanni suddenly calls to the house from the end of the courtyard, just where the inlaid stones touch the grass. His eyes gleam from under his mat of curly grey hair, and he stands half-turned, grinning, posing for a picture.

'Pretty morning!' he says at last, nodding and taking a deep breath. 'First rate! Sun, a good little wind, not too cold – fine hunting!' He gives a tug on the strap of his shotgun and straightens his shoulders, very male, very sure with his grey hair blowing. A hunter.

'Many days without you, Yanni. How's life?'

'All right, it is,' he laughs, but checking first, always alert for any little slight. Then his look lifts clear and straight again. 'And with you, I see, it's all right too. The way the money is, you *livéndi*, Yakovo, you fine one – why, that's how life goes for you as well!'

'No, unfortunately,' I say.

'It is, it is! You're saying I don't know?' He closes his eyes on me and makes his odd clicking laugh. He takes up my newly-shafted axe that's been soaking in the water ditch all week. He dries it on his shirt and gives it a rap on the cobblestones to see if the head shifts.

'No good, friend Yakovo! Look!' he calls, '*Yi*, Yakovo! Come out! I brought your money! Come have a cigaro! What are you doing, you big queer, you miser? Hiding? Podding peas? What news? *None*? Don't you have a radio? There's news! Certainly! You know it too, you liar! I can't make you out – never talking. Come here! You'll wake up!

42

No more ribbons-and-flowers writing for you! You'll learn the news soon! Or else it's going to eat you!'

And from then on, Yanni is around every day. No explanations ever come from him. He's simply back, hunting everywhere he goes again, with his shotgun ready and his dog Ektor running with him. He shoots his largest sparrows right in the brush between the road and the sea, where everyone else, Kristo and his American bird-whistle included, comes back empty-handed. Sometimes his gun roars too close to the house and the shot falls around us like hail.

'What is this, a war?' Manoli stands up from the stone by the spring with his hands on his hips. 'Do I need a war here?'

'He hunts . . . and he hunts . . . ey, what else? . . . meat, now, at forty drachmas a kilo. . . .' Maria sighs consolingly in their field while the shots ring out overhead with whistlings and crashings in the leaves, the old dog baying and churning past with his ears down.

One Sunday in March, I paid Yanni to help me make a window in the kitchen. We'd propped up the crossbeams so the roof wouldn't fall, and we were lifting the big stones out of the wall one at a time.

He barely watched what we did, as if he was just putting in time with the work until something better would happen. He moved mechanically with his thoughts somewhere else, saving himself up. I liked working with him. He was sure and cat-quick – I liked to see his hands forcing things as he looked away gravely. He never asked me about myself.

He'd hung his gun from the arbour outside. Ektor sat watching us as long as he could, trying in his hunting-dog way to stay aloof from my Katina's lickings and warblings. Finally he wandered around the side of the house with his nose to the ground.

Almost at once there were two cracks of a pistol and a yelp. Yanni listened for a moment, then he dropped down into the courtyard and went off at a run. An hour went by and it began to rain. I took his shotgun inside.

'Another sheep lost!' Manoli's Kristo called to the house queerly, standing white-faced by the bamboo fence with his hair in his eyes. 'Dog still eating him when I got there ... what could I do? Last week, a chicken–'

'And Yanni now?'

'Ey, the old uncle is crying about it.'

'Yakovo. A shame about Ektori, a shame, a shame, a shame,' Espasia said sadly, rightfully, in the morning when she brought me some eggs in a string bag. 'And now no dog for Yanni,' she sighed. Usually she leaves her gifts on the kitchen table.

Another day, Espasia comes to the house big with anger. Incredibly, Yanni has refused to help again. 'It's possible,' she mimics his low voice, turning down the corners of her mouth. '*Bori!* It's *possible* I'll help with your planting!'

Yanni takes and takes and gives nothing. All Manoli and Espasia have is the difficulty of him. If the stick-gate is left open and the sheep go wandering down the coast, or if a melon is stolen from shopkeeper P. Arkilaki's field across the road, or if only half the water is coming down the sluiceway, it's always *ta Yannachia*, the little Yanni's busy again.

'Yanni!'

'Ey!' the call comes back deep and hostile, positioning.

Manoli stands rigidly outside the field in front of the house while Yanni's goat frolics from furrow to furrow, dragging his spliced rope behind him. Maria's trying to snag the knotted end under her shoe, cooing, 'Come, sweet, come, our joy.'

Yanni's Mikalis stands by the gate with his hands behind

him. His four brothers are in Sydney, and at times like this he feels that far away too.

'Take the goat!' Manoli tells Yanni, who walks up slowly.

'Get the rope!' Yanni barks at Maria.

'Now!' she says.

Maria licks her lips and hops after the tether again. 'Come, beauty. We'll go cut some clover. Come, we'll go eat.'

'A hundred times, this way with your goat,' Manoli says, spreading his hands with a little jump.

'Goat's hungry ... old rope, for sure ... woman can't tie it,' Yanni nods in agreement. 'Boy just watches. Quick, Mikali!' he bellows, livid, searching the ground for a club.

'That's for you,' Manoli says. 'Does that have to do with me? My lentils, you see, are mostly ruined. You and I are finished here!' He dusts off his hands and starts away.

'All right. We'll fix it,' Yanni calls after him, but he doesn't go along pleading. The goat stops to watch too, and Maria snatches up the rope. She rubs his nose and ears. She winks and feels his fat stomach with her fingers.

Manoli jerks his head upwards: 'No! We're done! All gone by!'

But at my Name Day party two weeks later, there's Yanni back again, dancing seriously on the cobbles in his white knee-boots, slapping a heel as he drops down, rising and turning on the red bandana Maria holds for him. She giggles and shuffles her feet up and back, keeping time for him with her bird-shoulders bunched together.

And Manoli looks on from the best kitchen chair, listening to a little of what each person is saying, pleased to have company here at his old house.

The government has changed again and a garrison of soldiers has moved into Paleochora. These sombre mornings, Yanni walks from group to group along the street with a revolver tucked under his belt. He watches and listens while the police sergeant explains the Liberation to the clusters of angry faces.

Some wild-looking men down from the Pelikano mountains spin the sergeant dangerously back and forth, shouting questions at him. P. Arkilaki hides in his shop. Crazy Panayoti has his hat turned backwards, laughing and shooting with his fingers, not knowing a thing. But Yanni stands apart, merely waiting, holding the top of his greatcoat together.

'Chickens, they eat, the soldiers!' Kristo says. 'You think they pay for them? Bah! Yesterday, the baker cooked twenty pans of chickens for them. They take what they want from us.'

'And we eat,' Yanni laughs quietly and shrugs.

'We won't eat bread,' I say. 'Yesterday, Manuso couldn't bake any.'

'They're not taking Yanni's chickens, the old uncle's chickens,' Kristo says. 'Why? He hasn't got any.'

A west wind came on Christmas night and destroyed the fields right and left along the road. Yanni's furrows had been small enough to cover with branches.

Today he lies on his side with one eye open, wrapped in his coat, waiting under a carob tree for all the water to come down the sluiceway from the river.

'Very lazy,' Manoli says, looking around the side of the house. 'Very ugly, the way he sleeps and waits there.'

THE TOWN

THERE IS NO VISIBLE REASON FOR THE TOWN. ITS reasons and shapes have come and gone many times over. Now one peninsula is left a wilderness of shingle and gale-twisted cedars, while the next, longer one is crammed with the square white houses of Paleochora.

The mountains begin behind the green and yellow fields on the little plain, across which the dirt road to Chania, the capital city, turns north under a lane of tattered eucalyptus trees. On the rectangular bluff at the end of the peninsula a rust-coloured Venetian fortress overlooks the low-built town, which stops and starts in knots of ruined and inhabited houses and finally lurches up past the blue-domed church, ending in a tumble of overlapping mud roofs and bamboo enclosures.

To the east and west, the hills drop sheer again on the deserted coastline, with only the vastness of blue-black sea and the faint tipped ramp of Gavdos Island lifting just under the horizon, quarter-way to Africa.

When I first came here, the town had only three main suppliers: Pavlo the fruitman, who share-cropped his family properties near the mountain village of Anythri; Manoli's Kristo, who climbed all over the round hills of Selinou province in his motorcycle-taxi with whimsical orders like typewriter paper and legal stamps; and the irrepressible Herakles-Olympos cement boat, which crawled up on the skyline once a month, spent a lonely night by the pier and then sailed on around the headland to Cythera.

There were no gifts in Paleochora. There were inflicted exchanges. If I gave a man a hunting puppy or a paper cone of cucumber seeds, he had to give me something like a bottle of olive oil or a sack of almonds.

Useless and unnecessary gestures were always suspect, always insulting, and almost always given back. It was a happiness, almost a relief, to find that most wants were the same. Everyone knew what you wanted, which was a more or less selfless way to live.

Paleochora means Old Village. The bleak countryside around it still made each person in the town important to the next. Relationships were clear, cooperation was good. You had to have a plougher as a friend, and he was entitled to about one fifth of your next crop and at least one large, dignified meal. And somehow it ended up that things were still stacked in favour of the poor man – or the late man, or the hurt man. Not so that he weakened from expecting gift-like exchanges, but people were simply on his side. The only price was a kind of over-familiarity by the donor.

In P. Arkilaki's shop, an item for ten drachmas would drop inexplicably to eight for the person standing next to you. No one looked up or said anything, and Arkilaki went on weighing flour and cutting cheese. No one felt bad. But another day, after a good harvest or a money-filled letter from relatives overseas, the same man would be offended:

'Why eight? Ten, it says!'

Of its own, Paleochora would keep two cobblers, but not three; one olive oil mill, but not two. It took another kafenion over a tool shop, and a gunsmith over a notary.

Everything seemed to fall into permanent niches, even the goods in the stores. Week after week, month after month, each shop concentrated on one or two things: knives, brushes, pins, incense, candles, nails, toilet paper, cologne, matches, material, rat traps and rope.

Every summer in Paleochora was always the hottest in fifty years, and no one could ever remember a colder winter than the present one. The same houses were flooded, the same fields of the same crops were washed away, burned dry or gobbled up in the night by hedgehogs, and then planted again with the same insect stubbornness. The same people were driven back home by the heat and the cold – the shepherds, the charcoal burners, the beekeepers, and the family in the mill in the canyon.

Yet somehow each day was different. A pig could break loose during a church procession. A morose mule might clear out a kafenion. Now and then lost foreigners came magically out of the canyon from Chania. And each spring the gypsies came scavenging, selling, and stealing back their broken-down donkeys and mules. They came at the end of the winter, annually proving that a better season was almost here.

There were deaths: the open coffins were carried through the town, with Tasoula the Mourner pulling her hair and wailing behind. There were baptisms and weddings, ten or twelve a year, splendid, long brawls of eating, singing and dancing, the groom weeping and passing his hat, and the guests emptying their guns through the windows and ceilings. There were newspapers. Gambling was legal at New Year.

There was always a good spread of viewpoints in Paleochora. Many people, including myself, had come from some other, even worse place, bringing his own loyalties and sources of news. Everything was arguable, nothing was wholly, coldly solved. On Saturdays, men down from Anythri would go to their kinsman Yorgi's kafenion, where the flies were humming in the cool and there were the rich smells of mountain onions, coffee and tobacco. The loud Mazans and Spanyakans went to Kosta's place and sang their own songs and broke his plates. Baker Farthi's mother was stolen down from Hajibey, so naturally the simple, cautious exchanges and greetings to that village could be conveyed only at his shop, not through baker Manuso, the Gavdos immigrant.

Farthi would also have a few bright scarlet saddle blankets and woven goods from the Pelikano valley to sell. But only Manuso could offer you the turkeys and cedar nuts that came on last week's motorboat. Connections prospered, ties grew.

Feuding was the only real block to my everyday marketing. Family and personal differences were as well known as they were irreparable. But no one would tell you about them, or whose side your landlord or your baker was on. You merely felt strange in a new shop, as though you were too big for it. The personality was different. Things weren't in the right places. Everybody went quiet.

Then steadily you got a feeling for where you should go. You soon saw you should never divide haircuts, say, between Thefteri and Prokopi, or leatherwork between yourself and Andreas. I simply did without the things P. Arkilaki didn't have in his store.

When I came to Paleochora, I took on Manoli's social course – a wider one than most, including two of the ten kafenions, Manuso, the carpenter Eftiki, Priest Steliano and the mayor's mother.

I remember the day everything changed. I'd taken a slow walk to Anythri one afternoon and was coming back down the zig-zagging path into the canyon when I saw a group of men arguing on the road by the mill.

'Cuckolds cut the water,' Kristo called.

'Who did?' I asked him with my hand.

'That's it, who?'

The waterline that runs from the river to the town had been cut at exactly noon. Maybe it wasn't cut, maybe it had just broken. No one ever knew.

Now they were moving confusedly among the boulders and trees in ant-like clusters, some working simply, singly, cutting trenches through little gaps in the rocks, others fighting a long piece of timber back and forth like a battering ram with a sort of regular jump. And some were still talking and smoking by Kristo's motorcycle, which was angled off the road under a fig tree.

In the end no one found the pipe, and it was getting dark. When they all trailed back into the town in the twilight, the street was bustling with soldiers.

The last vehicle to enter Paleochora that week was the old maroon and grey bus from the Pelikano, which staggered in long after dark. Pappa Steliano and the Singer Sewing Machine man got out and made for the first house, just as the six town policemen began to patrol the street with torches, closing the doors and latching the shutters from outside. Heavy trucks came and left during the night.

When I rode into town in the afternoon, the bells were ringing and the police were moving back and forth through a crowd, slicing it up, shrugging good-naturedly and calling answers over their shoulders. Many times I heard the little sergeant explain, 'I'm from Lasithi! It's just the same over there – roads cut, trees down. I've just called Lasithi! We've got to wait and see.' And then, as I say, people started to push him and shout questions.

'Yakovo.' Yanni called me over to where he was standing in his greatcoat. But he said nothing else. He listened for a while and then walked away down the back street to his house.

The northern accents of the soldiers playing football in the schoolyard drifted down the street all afternoon. 'Where are they from?' people asked. 'Many soldiers! Are they ours?' Some said, *'Pelopponnesi!'* Others guessed NATO. *'Apo oli!* From everywhere!'

Two of the stores were allowed to open for an hour. The little sergeant strode into E. Kukuzaki's queerly arranged shop where I was labouring, without help, to find something for lunch. The sergeant ordered that all the gunpowder and shot be taken off the shelves and loaded into street sweeper Evangeli's wagon, which had drawn up outside, the donkey Omorfa dropping his ears at each new tone of voice.

'Happy hour!' the policeman wished me, turning smartly with a half-salute. 'Come to Paleochora only once a day at this same time. And not for long. Do you understand?' I asked him why, and E. Kukuzaki dropped under the counter to get the shot. The sergeant blinked and repeated slowly, 'Do you understand? Good.'

When I passed the cemetery wall and stopped to look back at the town, the police were coming out again, trying the doors and looking in all the empty houses. I thought, 'It's true. The world can go crazy.'

The second morning, more new rules followed: no groups of over five; no breaking plates when happy; seven o'clock curfew bells to be rung by Pappa Dimitri, the mountain priest; no evening promenade; no leaving town; no night fishing; no fishing from the pier; in fact, no fishing at all.

The sergeant should have included no listening to the shortwave set at Yorgi's kafenion, because Radio Cairo boomed all day in an unanswerable, high-pitched shout. Everyone knew they were lies: it was Radio Cairo. But there had to be some explanation for all this, even a hint would do. The stations in Athens were garbled, though even in the best of times the news was hard to understand from this far away.

The King was evidently back in power. Then the Air Force took over. Later still it was the Anarchists. Little chimes rang between each improvement. The Turks had taken a bite of Cyprus and the American fleet was sailing back and forth off Salamis, ready to back up anyone else who could save America's things in Greece. Absurdities.

Yorgi drew in his chin and made a few circles in the air with his hand. 'Nothing!' he said; seemed preoccupied. 'Yakovo. Sit down here and tell me what they're saying. Can't understand anything, bad luck ... only Cairo, now....'

From each stop on the dial came an angry stutter of voices, martial music, shouting, chanting. Some foreign stations came in as clearly as a voice from across the street, others through a whine of great distance, fading, rolling back.

'Turkey, that,' I offered.

'Israel,' Yorgi guessed. 'What's this?'

I listened for a moment.

'War everywhere,' Stelio the bus driver said, slapping his knees. Like the Singer Sewing Machine man, he'd left his razor up in Chania.

'Listen, now!' Yorgi bent closer, tuning in exactly. *'Englesiká!'* he said. *'Englesiká* for Yakovo to understand.'

'... here's the wind-up ... coming down....' There was a loud crack and a roar like the wind. 'Long drive ... Orvietto back, back....'

'Army radio,' I said.

'He says the Army radio! The Army radio, he says!' A circle gathered around the table, worried, self-centred, cowardly.

'... the Moose'll rattle the boards for ya, all right ... had a notion about that one, Buddy.... Looked like the long trip, all right, Jack.... Here's manager Bill Rigney to the mound ... mighty lonely li'l place to be sometimes, buddy boy....'

'Just talking,' I said.

When Yorgi carried the radio away, there were new sounds outside – footfalls, a child crying, chickens scratching by the door, the short slapping of the waves and the wireless clicking in the stationhouse.

In the warm, thundery afternoon, Kristo walked out to the house to tell me that Lykurgo and the Nikiforo of the olive mill were in jail. So were ten others up in Hajibey.

'Why?'

'Maybe Communists,' he said.

He told me that things looked bad and I should leave while I could. He said he'd take me around the west coast to Kristokilitisa Monastery in Kissamou province, where he knew the head priest. Then I could walk on to Espasia's village near Kastelli and stay there for a while.

I wasn't leaving. The coming hadn't been important enough. Kristo shrugged: he wanted to do what he could for me. I asked him where Yanni was. Katina barked the whole time.

That same evening, the road past the house was filled with riders. The few I knew were from Anythri, Maza and Rodovani. The others were from higher places, with sheepskin coats and multi-coloured woven knapsacks and saddle bags. A lone man would rock by first, his red and black saddle rug showing through the carob trees, then a string of mules bristling with rifles and shotguns that were roped in bundles like firewood. Some of the guns were old flintlocks with scoop muzzles, others of sleek, flat Italian makes. There were German guns from the war, Mausers and Stens, and rings of black pistols wired together. Each had a tag with a name.

I watched for a long time. Finally, one old full-bearded man rode by with black ballooning breeches and knee-boots. He had a rifle across his back and a dark headcloth twisted down over his eyes. Slowly he swung past the spring and took the lower track along the beach, cocking his head back to see, looking straight ahead without a word.

It seemed like all the guns in Selinou were spread across the floor of the stationhouse a few days later when I climbed the stairs for a reconsideration of my residence permit.

Corporal Lazaro proudly said that the bus was going through again, one every three days. There was a little stop and, ey, a little change in Rodovani, then I could go right on to Chania. Just tell them ahead of time how long I planned to stay, where, why, etc.

'Listen, Yakovo, soon it will be the same,' he said mock-confidentially, leaning forwards from his empty typewriter. 'Better!'

'Karamanlis will come. Or Papandreou,' said someone else in city clothes who was sitting in the corridor by the glass case of machine-guns. 'Which one do you like?'

'It's all right, Yakovo. Don't be afraid,' the corporal said. 'Good fellow!'

'Bad fellows, though, it's a fact. . . .' The city man lifted his shoulders and bobbed his hanging moustache, '. . . ey, maybe kaput.' The folding gesture of his hand was someone shot. I swallowed and Corporal Lazaro began to giggle. He made a few quick trigger motions with his one long fingernail and then shook it at me admonishingly: no, these things were rare. Two other officers rose from their cots in the next room and sat down backwards on chairs along the wall, grinning, alert, Greek. But the little sergeant opened his door and waved me in.

He sighed when we sat facing one another. He shifted right and left on his chair and made his banana-smile.

'You do what, Yakovo?'

'I write,' I said.

'Write what, Yakovo?'

'Notes for a book.'

'Of politics.'

'No.'

'Then?'

There was a pause.

'Amerika? Amerika?'

I nodded yes, wondering at it myself.

'Amerika. *Polá leftá*. Lots of money.'

He rubbed his thumb and forefinger together, then returned them to his chin.

That was half the interview. Before initialling and stamping my papers, however, the sergeant said,

'Yakovo. Now we don't like beards.' And he tipped the permit back in his hand. Happily, I hadn't reached for it.

I explained that I'd had a beard for years and that I wouldn't shave it off.

The sergeant tapped his fingers on the desk. It was all a little new to him.

'Shorter, then,' he snapped with a look sideways. The guns kept clattering down on the wooden floor in the hall.

I said no.

'Yes! You will,' he said. 'You'll shave.'

'I'll leave.'

'Ah-h? Where will you go?'

'I don't know,' I said.

The sergeant took a pencil in his hands and looked out of the window at the long arch of the coastline in the sun and the road disappearing into the mountains. He would notify me about this shortly, he said. He would send word out to the house. Then he gave me permission to go on living here.

Only a handful of foreigners have filtered down to Paleochora since then. Two smooth, young Dutchmen in yellow came for one evening and then went away. And there was the wind-crazed German archaeologist, Eberhart, who had been in the mountains the whole time. And Stefano-or-Steve, who came back from Pittsaburgi in a new brown suit. He told me there'd been some trouble lately in Chania and everyplace, but that he sure didn't know. At last in December, when Paleochora lay shivering in the coldest north wind in hundreds of years, came a glimpse of another beard – a thick, full one, like heather, like St Paul's when he visited the town once too. Priest Steliano whispered that we might not be pulled into barber Thefteri's after all.

The guns went back to the villages, and a three-week hunting season was declared. The first newspapers showed the King standing on the palace steps with his new military cabinet. The same picture ran for several days, taken from different sides. Then Radio Cairo said that the King had gone to Rome. Then to Paris. Then home, further and further away.

The mail came again on a Friday, I remember. Niko the postman waved madly from the road, blew his whistle and handed me a telegram: WHERE ARE NOBODY; KELHEP. Puzzling.

Life has been very quiet since I have decided to stay – no other news or cables, no motion or changes at all. The days go on about the same as before, here close by the house. Sofia brings her new kittens in from the woodpile. Morris goes on making his heaps in the courtyard. I have the pleasant feeling of being in control and holding my things together just by living here.

But in the town I notice that flint lighters are now illegal, giving a free field to the government Monopclió matches, which Crazy Panayoti sells in the post office for two drachmas a box. And there's a law that all houses and stables must look prettier. Now, after a few days' work, Paleochora flows solid, sparkling white from the mouth of the canyon out to the tip of the peninsula. Probably the town hasn't looked so new in 3000 years. Every low flat-roofed house and shop, every ruined wall and even the trunks of the mulberry trees along the empty street are bright white.

'Because, you see, so few foreigners come now,' Yorgi repeats like a verse. His long-handled whitewash brush drops down into the pail and spatters up again.

Life goes on. P. Arkilaki's Yanoula has had her baby. Evangeli is sweeping the street again. The Singer Sewing Machine man is back. The little foreign industrial leaflets which have been delayed up in Chania now sit out in serious, glossy stacks all over Paleochora for people to read about the development of the island.

And every day about noon a lone silver plane drones high over the waiting town and out towards Gavdos, where it banks south-east into the clouds doming slowly, mightily over the headland.

MANOLI

A HUGE RAMPART MASSES SILENTLY OVER THE SUNNY tundra, dark and unreal against the blue. Lighter clouds roll up to its edge like white surf and crumble slowly down, tumbling out over the dry hills and the winding road in the canyon.

The shadow of winter falls like doom across the olive groves and the long town on the peninsula, and with it an old sense of solitude and depth comes over the dimming landscape. There's a continuous whispering. The sparrows hop from branch to branch.

The waves are rising from nowhere with a grumbling of stones down the empty beach. Morris circles on his rope, about to bray, looking out through a gap in the trees. There's a roll of thunder, and Willy the goat walks to the open door and turns his head questioningly.

Another breath of cold, and a malevolent, waiting stillness. Katina lies in the courtyard facing the window where I'm writing with the gladness and terror of being alone. She cocks her ears and glances from side to side as the large, warm drops tip the carob leaves and spatter up the dust around her.

Soon the first rain is falling hard like ramrods, splashing up in a mist from the courtyard stones and the oven dome.

The frogs begin to sing in the brittle yellow stubble in the sluiceway. Everywhere, the dips and holes fill with water, and then the fields start to flow.

'Rain, Yakovo!' Manoli's Espasia billows across the field towards the house, laughing and tying on her black shawl. 'Down it comes! Down it comes!'

We peer under the dripping eaves at the hunched wood-cutters trooping back to town. Espasia looks up at me like a little black owl.

'*Good* for the trees, it is! *Good* for the grass!' And after a while she goes out into it again, wandering away through the grove, watching everything drink.

Morris nods along behind me down the path to his ruined hut under the cliff. I scythe some grass for him and give him his half-pail of rye in a corner under the fallen timbers and hanging blocks of sod. Then I see the angry sky in the door, and I pour in the whole sackful.

Going back, the house looks dark and still, hidden in the whorls of trees ahead, dead-looking, except for the orange curtains blowing from the windows like sails.

I carry the lanterns into the kitchen and sit at the table listening to the long, tapering gusts of wind clattering the bamboo fences. It seems a long way over the mountains to the big, safe towns on the north coast.

In the morning, the walls are shimmering with the sunlight on the water outside. But it's still raining, and a new wind is running in from the sea. The sun is a perfect red sphere over the path to the spring, changed and dim, set back in the sky, unrelated. The house feels different today, as if it's another year.

Yanni smiles and shakes his spread fingers downwards, walking erectly with his gun to the canopy of the plane trees in the turn of the road. My buckets run over without a sound while we talk and exchange cigarettes.

'Still raining, Yakovo,' he says, turning in his lips and blowing out a breath. 'Two days now,' he nods.

'We'll wash into the sea.'

Yanni clicks his laugh, 'Not yet, not yet. Bah! The rain's good.'

He tells me the gypsies have come, many of them. They've camped under the mill.

'Early,' I say.

'Certainly, early,' Yanni frowns. 'I don't know why. Now they'll freeze.'

And he tells me Manoli's sick again. Which brings back all the hopelessness of the town in the winter – the slaughtering post on the beach, the whistling power wires, the woodsmoke from the bakery blowing in over the roofs along the muddy back street. I can see Manoli grinning in his bed again, gesturing for me to sit by the brazier, foolish and useless under the lit ikons in his cement room. I can't go into town today. It's Sunday too, no chance of letters or food.

Yanni goes on up the road and picks his way into the dark green brush behind the sluiceway.

The day begins to pass. The storms drive in from the north one after the other, as though an infinity of clouds and cold were there. I try writing again, but I feel tired and stuffed under all my clothes. I can't really get warm, and I can't really write. I leaf through what I've done, and I realize that though I have tried to make this a story, there doesn't seem to be one. It's a pity, because it would be so easy to read. Possibly things were wider and more serious than I thought. Otherwise, why would I already feel differently about them? I can't seem to write to include what happens later on and how I'll be. It's as if I have no steady currents of my own, and just the details of the place to tell me things.

I look out at the lemons hanging like Christmas lights in the gloom. The rain falls down mindlessly, spattering against the glass, threatening me, scattering the years behind until only this wet room is left. I hum a little mountain tune, but how can it be happy with the miserable gulls calling?

At noon I take Morris down to the bridge at the river. A hollow tree has fallen across the road during the night. Already a faint track climbs up around it along a rock shelf and drops down again through Manoli's vineyards, where the rows of bare cut vines are writhing in the water. I ride on under the chaos of fast-moving clouds with my hands rolled in my coat, remembering the summer hills crackling in the heat-haze and the dream-like roaring of the cicadas.

For eight months the river has run in a rivulet through the deep pools and dry piled stones under the bridge. Now it's raging up close under the wooden planking, and the wall-tops of the fields across wind away like pathways through the flooding water. Willow bushes and heads of gorse drift by. An olive log crashes into the bridge supports with a thud, hangs motionless for a moment, capturing a little eddying calm, then suddenly it vaults over-end and darts weightlessly away at a sickening speed. The island is washing into the sea – a band of brown water slants out from the coast into a grey void.

Yanni's right. Five tall tan gypsy tents are standing in the rocks under the millhouse. Two white mules and a donkey with beads are tied to a rope between the trees, and behind them a cart is let down on its shafts.

'Gypsies!' Maria will call to the house, wide-eyed, de-lighted. 'Take your clothes off the line today! You harvest your cucumbers, they harvest your clothes!'

The gypsies are something superimposed on the place, not quite solid, not quite clear. They're either here, behind things, or else on their way, sending their mystery ahead:

another delicate way of life going on quietly, separately, the whole time.

I wonder why they've come in January. Yanni didn't know either. Was it so hard up in the north that even here seemed better? The field policeman and the olive pickers have gone back to town – everyone has, even the three army surveyors taking notes and walking over walls with their poles and strings. On all the plain there's only this little mist of smoke over the peaked tents, the life in them seeming so small and cold.

Morris tics and shivers in the downpour with his ears parted flat, not really seeing anything as he uses his life up. I wonder how many years are left in him. Three? Five? It actually depends on how I treat him. 'Grandfather, this one! Look out, he'll die on the road today!' they say in town when they stop me and pull open his eyelids and his mouth.

I've just called him Morris. But what is this obstinate strand of life from his head down his gouged back to his tail, and how long can it last, balanced in the winter on such spindly legs? He opens the kitchen latch with his lips and stands looking in at the food scraps on the floor. He hunches himself tense when I try to push him. He stiffens his neck and his knobby knees to make himself heavier and more difficult to move. Everything seems sad today – I'm going back home. Left alone, Morris probably wouldn't go to town either.

No one's come while I was away. Things are just as I left them. My notebooks are stacked, the lanterns are ready for the night. My walking stick and my red wool shirt are still hanging on the back of the chair. My paraffin bottle and my tins of lentils and oil look up and ask me, 'Now what will you do?'

In the window, the twisted arbour posts and the carobs along the road shine in the evening glow. The little medlar tree in the middle of the field is pinned back in the wind, fluttering hard, while the armies of white and grey clouds drive massively over, sealing out the last light.

The winter has come down over the disappointment of the year, condoning it. This must be how time passes. It goes coldly by in a block with the wrong still sealed inside, until finally a year drops away. You belong to whatever takes you, because time is on its side.

I feel the great cloud-shapes of the day still reaching over this square house in the clearing. The boulders and trees on the hill sweep upwards and stretch together, hanging out over me.

I listen and wait at night. For what? The wind moans, but nothing else is coming. I could go off walking all night again, past the grave-lights in the cemetery, through the hive of sleeping white houses and up into the mountains. Should I stay here in Manoli's old room, or should I walk in the dark until dawn, splashing home again in the rain with Katina, looking for my light in the trees?

The lantern flames flicker over double, one under the wall of shelves, one here on my table. It's as if there's no house at all tonight and the wind is passing right through.

In the morning a fine, wet mist is falling noiselessly. Manoli is chopping stakes in the hut behind the sluiceway where he keeps his field tools. The door is propped against the fig tree by the wall. When I stop and listen on the path to the spring, I hear his muttering and short catches of breath.

I see his hobnailed boots and then his black coat and his narrow white face in the darkness. He holds perfectly still until I start towards him. Then there's a motion inside and another piece of wood rattles into the corner. Manoli sits on the hay with outstretched legs, waiting for me. A match flares up.

'Good morning, Yakovo! I'm working. Yesterday I was sick.'

'Come inside the house; I'll make some tea,' I say.

'No, must finish a few stakes first . . . all the rain, now . . . sheep penned up three days. . . .'

The fig tree dips insanely in the wind as I stand looking in the doorway. Manoli takes up another cut branch, chops its end to a point and throws it over his shoulder. The saddle frame, the rim of the flour sifter and the light handles of the hoes lift out from the smoke-blackened walls around him. The big and little seed crops glow back in a line on the clay floor.

'It's cold here, though.'

Manoli shrugs. 'Ey, winter. What can we do?'

So I go back to the flooded kitchen and start working mechanically again. Crete! Crete is Paleochora. Crete is the coast. Crete is only this wet box-house where I live by myself. I clear the drains under the doors with a rod, and nail blankets over the north windows to keep out the wind. Sofia mews at the slightest sound of a cup and a spoon. Katina's skulking underfoot, ducking irritatingly back and forth to miss my boots, cringing because I hit her with a frying pan once.

The hours pass and another terrific deluge lashes down through the floating veils of rain. A branch snaps somewhere outside and skims across the roof. Crete is a coincidence.

Andreas the cobbler cups his hands over his eyes and peers into the window with a burlap sack on his head. 'Open up!' he calls, yanking the goat bell on the door. He's torn it loose by the time I lift the latch. 'What's this?' he says, and tosses it tinkling out in the grass by the amphora for the worthless object it probably was.

'Po-po-po! Where's your woman?' Andreas groans as he looks from the sagging bamboo ceiling to the streams of muddy water running down the walls. Another man with baggy riding breeches plastered to his legs sloshes in behind him in laceless boots. Still another follows, scowling, exhausted, with a dripping brown army jacket wrapped around his head like a turban. Manolı stops chopping outside.

'Bridge is broken!' Andreas says, shaking Willy from the chair and sitting down with a crash. 'Fifty-two years old, I am, and I've never seen rain like this!'

'Andreas!' Manoli calls, muffled. 'What, with the bridge?'

'Down, the bridge!' Andreas shouts with a cut of his hand. 'Bitten off!'

'Did you see Espasia?' the voice strains. 'Eh?'

'Manoli?' Andreas asks me, pointing to the window.

Manoli calls again, 'Espasia, I say!'

'No one, no one! Dead sheep! Dead mules! Where are you, old man?'

'What's happened to the gypsies?' I asked him.

'Everything's gone!' Andreas shouts, unhearing. 'Two days, maybe three, before you can ride across there again!'

'A week,' agrees the turban man, filling my room with himself.

'What will you do now?' barks the voice from the hut.

'What will we do? We'll go to the canyon bridge! And then we'll get home!' says Andreas. 'Where is he? Where's Manoli? Why doesn't he come out?'

'The bridge is far,' I say.

'Ey-hey – ?' they all shrug.

I dully picture the square-faced bus from Chania with its fenders flapping and its open motor jumping, its loudspeaker blaring music as it switches down to the low span of concrete with its monument-shrine: THE KING BUILDS ... 1951 ... FOR PEOPLE OF PALEOCHORA. It seems five miles to the bridge, but maybe by going over the mountain....

'*Yi*,' Andreas spreads his arms helplessly, looking down at his soaked breeches and his knees peeping through like eggshells. The others shiver and rub their arms – and run into the rain again. I take a step towards the door, wondering if I'll go too.

When they've left, Manoli comes ducking around the fallen arbour and stands next to me, about as tall as my belt. We watch the trio drop jerkily over the grey ridge rocks on the hill.

Manoli lights one cigarette after another. He holds his glance away from me and laughs and agrees even before I speak. I lean back in my chair, somehow dreading the whole day with him, now that the bridge is down. He sits with his back straight and his hands on his knees, his tiny boots dangling a few inches above the floor.

An hour of silence goes by, then suddenly he walks out the door, calling back, 'I'm going to see the river, and maybe to go on to town.'

'Wait! We'll go together.'

So Manoli walks ahead of me with his axe in his belt and my brimmed cap perched on top of his head. He wears his black overcoat like a cloak, sliding and stumbling down the rutted road towards the river trees.

Whole sections of smashed fences are strewn haphazardly on both sides of us, showing the tipped corn stalks and the flattened furrows in the fields. Manoli stops with his hands on his hips and shakes his head. The goats are standing motionless at the very ends of their tethers, as close together as possible. We cut them loose one by one, and they walk slowly off through a break in the wall and up through the flowerless heather on the hill. We open the tin gate of the sheep pen, but somehow they've all gone away. Manoli throws his stakes in the bushes. He flicks his fingers out hopelessly.

And we go on to see the bridge. It's broken neatly on the far side, one slab of cement thrust upwards on end with its metalwork jutting out like teeth. Beyond, the water is even tearing at the cut-stone turn of the canyon road.

'They were about – there, the gypsies, the *tsigáni*,' I say, gesturing around the curve of the river to the pointed rocks under the mill.

'Ey?' Manoli starts and frowns. He slides down lower by the shining stones on the bank, crouching to see the town through the broken branches. After a few minutes we turn back to the evening at the house.

Manoli sits without a word. I move behind him quietly, filling and lighting the lanterns, thinking of nothing. He taps his axe on the chair and looks out at the crossing bands of rain in the twilight. I start some water boiling and take out two tin plates.

'Have you ever seen it rain like this before?' I ask him. It doesn't matter what I say any more.

Manoli clicks his tongue. No. The branches go on scratching the windows. 'Only ...' he clears his throat and sits back, 'Only during the war.'

I glance at his reflection in the glass. He never talks about the war. Kristo was his only son to survive it. Yanni told me how the Germans shot Manoli's Dimitri with thirty others against the wall of the mill. A year later, his Vasso's plough struck a leftover mine. Tasoula the Mourner told me she'd heard it all the way up in Spanyako. One of Espasia's old yellow photographs shows Dimitri holding his glass together with four or five others at Yorgi's kafenion, a half-moon of thick black hair hanging over his wild eyes. In another picture Vasso stands half-turned on the road by the bridge with a bound lamb over his shoulders, the plain hot and still behind him.

The drops on the window sparkle in the lantern light. Manoli's hand rises and falls on his knee, and he laughs softly.

'... had nothing, back then ...' he goes on after a while. He coughs and leans back with folded arms. 'They had us eating grass, like the goat there. There was an officer – Hans, Haz, do I know? Lieutenant, kapitano, what kind of an officer, I don't know ... he was a little stupid, the Hans. It was a long time ago. Rain coming down then? A lot!'

Manoli smiles and wipes his eyes. I carry over the steaming plates of wild celery and potatoes and put the lantern between us. He takes his fork in his knotted hand and pushes his food down the table with it, away from a roof-leak.

'One day, the Haz comes to the house – this house, when we were here. "Manoli! Give us your oil!" "Oil?" I say. "Eh, come! The oil you've hidden, the oil in the amphoras that were outside!" "All gone," I say. "I gave it to the priest."'

Manoli stiffens and purses his mouth, making a fist on the table, '"All gone? All gone? All? Ey, *gut, gut!*" And off he goes again, the Hans.'

Manoli sits straight, remembering. His ears barely show over the table I made. He throws his cigarette on the floor with a hiss and his toothless mouth twists into a grin.

Evidently, Kristo and he had sealed the oil amphoras with clay and buried them together with their shotguns in the lemon grove. Espasia sat on the roof to watch the road. The oil was safe until the day Hans came again with some Australian prisoners. Manoli sucks in his cheeks and holds his wrists together.

'"Manoli! Now I'm having my prisoners dig a trench here!" "Where?" "Across the field and through the grove." "Ey, difficult." "Difficult? Why difficult?" "Because you don't know where the ground is hard. And if you go into a soft place, you'll hit one of the old Turk walls and have to start over again." "Ah ... ah-h!" ' Manoli opens his mouth and winks. He taps his forehead with his fingers:

'Stupid! That stupid, he was!'

Manoli turns in his lips and cranes his face forwards with hooded eyes: ' "*Gut!* Show me where, then quickly! Here?" ' Manoli points to the stone sink. ' "Ey – ?" ' he shrugs. ' "There, then?" "Better over there," ' Manoli says. ' "I'll show you." ' He slaps the table with his hand and laughs. One shaky finger makes a zig-zag around his plate and his water glass.

'And his trench went so ... and so ... and so ... around the trees where the oil was and down along the path, only where I said ... only where I needed ditches. Even the one in front, where your dog sits. ...'

He shakes his head and looks past me with shining eyes. 'All gone now, though! Gone-by! It's a today-life, Yakovo,' he says. 'That's all it is.'

I lie awake listening to the doors beating and the lemons knocking on the walls. Slowly the room takes shape – the oblong table in the starlight, the slanting row of books, the loaded shelf. The lanterns are cold and empty.

It must be nearly dawn. Manoli's still in the house. He went to sleep on the kitchen table with his coat over him. I left him a candle in a cup.

The sound of mules on the road comes through the clear morning, fades, then holds steady. Neither louder nor softer; the slow, determined clicking of many hooves and the jingling and creaking of a cart, stopping, starting again with a splash and a whistle. More soft voices come along, and pass by.

It's January. The wind is from the west today. I can hear church bells and the river and the cocks crowing from the town.

WINTERFLOWERS

THEN THE CHICORY FLOWS AS BLUE AS WATER UNDER
the bushes and trees, pouring in more and more until a
flood of cerulean flowers spreads down the banks onto the
rutted road. Kristo and Corporal Lazaro weave through
them with the motorcycle-taxi, whirring in and out of gear
and grinding the horn on the sidecar as they pass the house.

It's grey weather, warm and damp. The winter grows
richer and darker until one day the anemones are glowing
in the shadows, smears and blots of colour bursting by the
path and tracing the tops of the broken walls. They cover
the roof of Morris's house, little cold fires of purple and crimson lighting the ground everywhere, parting over their
black-button centres without the sun, smelling of only earth
and rain.

But the old stone hills have no sheen of their own, no way
to receive life any more. This piling of winterflowers around
the erratic boulders is too clear and sudden. I almost don't
want to see it, because the bright rush of today-life isn't
accepted, isn't really taken in at all.

The heather and gorse fill the gullies with a hollow mantle
of violet and yellow that rolls and plumes over the hills until
only the ridge rocks are showing.

Espasia likes gorse best – the flowery fields and gorse. She stumbles up to the window and sees that I've already brought pots and baskets of orange-yellow into the damp, still room. So she heaps her armload under the open window. She's still out cutting more, black Espasia stooping by the vineyard wall with a sparkle of her knife. A little west wind carries the sweet resinous smell to sea, miles out from the house.

Each day of winter brings some change, some new level of colour, so strong that I'm struck by something like a memory, here where no one can see me or say otherwise. The year looks familiar when I hang the straw mats in the scraps of sun on the fig tree.

But I still won't follow the bright, uncertain life of winter-flowers – not the way I've followed the worlds of clouds, watching each friendly pink and green break in the sky, waiting for the landscape to lighten again. Not the way I watch these loose leaves catching on the cobbles by my door, whirling up and stopping again, fewer and fewer. I wait with them each time for the sudden calm I know is spring. Who could imagine how tired I feel?

Waves of tall poppies appear on the threshingfloor and under the carob trees, advancing bigger like paper-anemones. Bent over, they make it a narrow path, long red drops running into gross lakes of scarlet, with only blurrs and stubble underneath.

All over the poppy-covered fallow land, higher flowers are branching up – tiny yellow sparks of anise waving at the tips of their invisible stalks, blue bellflowers and tall nodding clusters of Easter lavender which Maria will come to cut for the bier of Christ.

A row of almonds blossomed in pink clouds deep in the grove, making a fresh background for this old stone house.

But when I walked back to them, the branches were already bare and strung with webs. The petals lay scattered in rings under the branches. They bank up at the end of the sluiceway, coming in from nowhere, as the olive trees go on blowing silver and dusky green over the muddy ploughed land.

The ledges and niches in the rocks are crammed with marigolds and golden crowns of crocuses, as though the whole spring is concentrated there, high, high up, hidden in the wind-stripped heather in the saddle of the hill.

It comes over me here how far away I really am, only for an instant, next to Katina in the shadow of the ridge. But far from what? What makes me think so? The carobs creaking over the path? The mottled sea? As I stroke Katina automatically, I know I've never wanted more from life than days like these. Is it fair to be so separate from this outraged world? Looking around me, I write in my notebook that my life is just single days, this small and bright. Yet is it too hard being alone in them? Is this what being alone is like? If so, then it's a little like nothing.

Dark maroon orchids grow apart from one another, some places having none of them at all. I want to forget, not remember. Otherwise, won't the same things happen? I can look back, but the past is so short and worthless that it fuses into a whole just before this moment – and suddenly beyond it, exactly as the thyme merges and moves upwards from the masses of shiny nettles. What is it that I know? When I think I've caught a glimpse of it, it's not there any more. When I come near to touch it, it's already going away, because I've taken something moving into my hands.

Again and again, I go straight to the same places through the stocky purple lupins – to the wild pear tree which has split a boulder on the ridge, to the tangles of mauve ebony hanging in the cold stream gullies, to the border of armless olives along the Turkish road turning out to nowhere from under the hill. But they're only feelings, not real places at all: not far places.

Manoli's field hut is still deserted and shut while the new speargrass is coming bright green across the vineyard and among the lemon trees flowering white by the wall. Gladioli appear between the roots and dark wet logs on the ground, opening little magenta swords from the top of the stems downwards, finally budding down low, unseen, in the blowing wheat.

This is just like the time I first came here, when the earth was struggling alive and already dying. Manoli led me back along the river to see his old house, ducking ahead through the lemon grove, deeper and deeper until the sea was lapping against the hills.

From the vineyard path I could only see the back of the house – not even that, but only a daisy-covered roof and a corner of cut stones. Katina nosed the cones of wild lilacs and found they were fresh. I looked at the morning glories heaped over the broken arbour, and I thought I'd never have to go on again.

Willy discovers the violets flowering too late between the courtyard stones. The little rock irises on their thick striped stems are gone from the feet of the olives. And the sad pink-washed asphodels behind the path walls are gone too: tall stalks with no blossoms. They're just like me – something in me rises and declares itself too, and always fades again, finding no confidence.

The sea currents wind south from their finished work, and only a spray of tiny white margaritas is flung behind, bunching around the beach rocks, powdering the bare mountains of the Pelikano with brief lights and shadows.

VASSILI

THE PATH BEGINS AT THE CHURCH OF THE EYELESS
Saints, a faint white groove worn across the drifts of slate
and margaritas, winding down the ridge and disappearing,
curving far below the silent mountainside into the olive trees
and red tile roofs of Vassilaki.

In the furthest bend of the path, three moss-covered chest-
nut trees lean out together to make a spot of shade in the
steep terraced fields. There is a spring high above, a trickle
of pink oleander dropping down through the boulders towards the great, full trees. The clear water sparkles into a
stone basin there, and a long silver dipper with a cross
glimmers at the bottom.

From here you look out over the lost little world of the
Pelikano, disintegrated into half a dozen crumbling white
villages jammed in the folds of the mountains – Tsaliana,
Vouta, Vassilaki, Hajibey; I don't even know all their names.

A river runs along the narrow valley floor, and patches
of fields tilt up the hillsides and run to points in the rock slides
and gorse. A tiny world of its own, shrunken back on itself
now, baffled by hardships. Only from up here can you see
all of it: the soul of the ancient place seems to be left by the
three trees and the dripping water. If you walk down to the

87

vendetta-cursed towns, the larger feeling vanishes. You come upon people too suddenly, catching them at their lives of neutral regularity. They're polite and welcome you with wine, but then they don't quite know what to do with you.

The *Pelikani* apologize for everything you see, whether it's a cockroach hole or a heavy maroon and red blanket on a loom. 'All bad,' they say. 'Whoa, friend! You've come a long way for a bad meal today! We eat bad, we drink bad – all bad!' they laugh, as if how they are is just a matter of money. The women whisper and giggle behind you and call the others to come and look, wild people from somewhere long ago. And after a while you think you're back there yourself, with no way home.

All around, over the outlying walls and beyond the stacks of blue bee boxes, there's a final, lonely stillness, as if all the different ages-past of the place will never take a definite shape

again. The sudden voices, the handgrips and the pounds on
the back are a little too hard, defiant, maybe mocking you.
They all down their glasses of wine, and it's fine. But when
you do, they say, 'He's drunk! Have some more!' I've found
it's better for me to stay away from Pelikano towns, merely
keeping the thought that all the time I'm down on the coast,
this ancient life gutters on here unseen.

So I sit very still in the mixed light of the trees when I
see the head and shoulders of a lone figure come up on the
path ahead. Let him go by, I say to myself.

He doesn't come nearer, though. He just waits there like
a sentry. Katina is watching him too. She whines and resettles
her chin between her paws. Her tail even wags, once, twice.
In the far distance a flock of goats spills over the slope with
a faint ringing of bells. Slowly I look back at the path dropping down from the honey-coloured church, tiny and perfect
against the blue. He must have seen me coming for a long
time. He wants me for something?

At last he makes a quick downward motion with his hand,
and so I stand up with my dog. When we go into the brightness towards him, he turns without a word or a greeting
and starts away again across a field with crosses whitewashed
on the boulders. Odd! I can't help smiling and walking faster.

He's tall and fair, dressed in a short army jacket and patched
woollen breeches bound at the boot-tops with burlap to keep
out the thistles. He goes ahead of me, bent, with his long
arms hanging at his sides, walking flatly, single-mindedly to
whatever it is he's done.

There is a little pile in the grass to one side – some green
artichokes and the gleam of a clasp-knife. Ducking down
from my glance, he takes up two or three in each of his big
hands and motions me to open my knapsack.

'Thanks!' I say. 'Enough!'

'*Che alo!* And more!' he sings, stooping for more.

'Enough.' I swing the knapsack over my shoulder and re-settle my hat, waiting, intrigued.

But the enormous hands appear again with a shake. *'Ap! Op!'* So off comes the knapsack again. In fact, he takes it away from me. Squatting, he crams in more and more around the edges until it's stuffed round and greedy with artichokes.

'Many,' I say.

'When they're good,' he says, rising and fixing his full hostile stare on me, 'then they're not many.' He turns his hand back and forth questioningly.

'Paleochora,' I tell him simply. Katina still sits at a distance looking off into space. Nothing alarming yet.

'Deutsch?'

'No.'

There's something separate and arrogant about him, very different. He turns down the corners of his mouth, baas and draws his fingers out under his chin, his manly red neck bursting from the drabness of khaki.

'For the winter, my beard,' I say.

He nods yes, and at the same time he makes the line of a hat across his forehead. *'Kapélla,'* he says. He also hates my brimmed hat.

'No?' I ask him. A donkey calls deep down in the valley. Katina sighs and rolls on her side.

'No?' he repeats.

'And who has planted all these artichokes?' I ask.

'I, all of them, all,' he says with queer concern.

We stand silently for another moment, looking out in different directions.

Then I turn and run away from him without looking back, taking long strides back up the hillside over the dead roofs of Vassilaki.

March has come, and Sofia dreams in the sun on the window

ledge, tipping her ears at the sounds of the donkeys carrying seeds and manure up the road. Katina yawns and rolls in the better weather. Johannes the bee is gone. I still find myself looking up for him.

One day, I decide I'll go to Chania. Espasia says she'll feed the animals:

'Go, Yakovo. I'm here! Go up and buy things!'

The bus ride north is a good change. The groves and wind-breaks fly by in a pleasant, sunny blur. Many flocks on the plateau. The Bishop of Kandanos climbs aboard with a ring on every finger. High, thin clouds today. I'm not sick once. I wonder whom I'll meet.

But things aren't right in Chania. We stop in a strange place, not by the tinsmith's anymore, and I'm the only one who is surprised. The market is empty, just a few lumps of tomatoes and some split cucumbers, no better than Paleo-chora's. Colonels and majors are out walking and saluting everywhere with their riding crops and their brown leather gloves, holding down their hats in the wind. And there's a sign:

IF YOU'RE A CLEAN MAN AND
A CHRISTIAN, THEN IT'S
IMPOSSIBLE TO BE A COMMUNIST

Soldiers are drilling in the square, filing by through the bands and flags and uneasy hand-clapping. The people I know look pale and worried; they touch their fingers to their lips before we talk. Then what is there to say? My days at home seem so unlikely. Have they been the same days as these?

The wind is blowing the water white in the harbour and rattling the panes of glass in the kafenions. I sit in the sun with my basketful of apples and fresh notebooks. All the other tables are bare. One old man rows in from his mooring and crouches on the stone stairs to the water, throwing a little grey octopus hand over hand on the pier with a *smack! smack!* sounding off the fortress walls and the arc of sagging wooden houses.

I leave on the bus the next morning at dawn, when the swallows are wheeling over the minarets. All the way back over the mountains, it feels like I'm seeing things for the last time.

Even in Paleochora I begin to sense something new – sort of a reckless gaiety, self-ridiculing, as though the town had been judged too remote and harmless, and had been passed over.

All day long people send Crazy Panayoti on sad, impossible errands. And there are loud voices on the street. '*Opa-op! Yi!*' Kristo and the ticket-taker from the bus are laughing and struggling stiff-legged. Grigori the blacksmith hobbles out and locks one of the tossing heads in his arms, steer-wrestles, whoops himself.

Pappa Steliano is smoking his chibouk alone under the tall window at Yorgi's. He keeps turning the pictureless pages of *Ta Nea*, glancing up and down at the big print first with a shine of his glasses, then creasing the sheets wearily and setting to again. The noon plane grumbles high overhead.

Today is St Konstantine's. There's a military celebration in town tonight. One, two, three coloured rockets sprout over the outline of flat roofs, and a fourth streaks out low and explodes over the water: silence all across the plain. Then a cock crows, and the donkeys begin to bray from the empty houses.

A march-band has come to play, and a general from Rodo-

vani will be here later to make a speech. A long row of tables
trails out the doors of Yorgi's kafenion, and across the street
is a string of lights with a sign painted on a sheet: THE
STRENGTH OF THE COUNTRY'S PEACE IS ITS MILITIA.

So far, only plates of sea-salt are arranged down the centre
of the sauce-spotted tablecloth. There will be something to
eat, but not much because the gathering is more important
than the food.

The places fill noisily with a smell of mothballs and
cologne. The chairs go regularly down the table sides to
about halfway, then there are crushes of people waiting
on planks between fish boxes, right down to the vacant place
of honour.

The band plays the same march back and forth over the
crowd with the cymbals crashing on and on, covering up
the trilling of a little violin in front. Then, as suddenly as
they came, the musicians rise with a clatter of music stands
and chairs, and a green bus backs down the street to get them.
From here, they go to Hajibey. It's rather horrible.

Thefteri the tailor sits in their place, looking too small with
only his lyra and his wine glass, playing the melancholy tunes
of 'Agrimi' and 'Captain Koumis'.

The charcoal smoke filters into the harsh light of the waiting scene. The sea rolls dully behind the joined house fronts.
Pappa Steliano is telling the reassuring story of the ninety-
nine saints hiding in the catacombs of Azogeri, pausing,
sighing, stroking his rectangular beard. A few bend to
hear him, but most of us turn and watch for lights in the
canyon.

'O-pah, Vassili!' someone calls. 'Welcome! Vassili from
Vassilaki!' All the faces look up grinning. I have to think for
a moment who this tall man might be, bringing his feet
together and returning an upside-down salute.

'What news, Vassili? Much snow up there?'

'Vassili! How are the turkeys? *Gobble-gobble!*'

'All right,' says the frowning giant, bowing slightly, looking at me over the stirring rows of heads with eerie gravity.
'All right.'

Vassili is dressed as he was that day in March. He kicks
a chair in for himself, his lighter khaki breaking a gap in the
line of black suits. Other voices call to him down the table,
leaning their round faces forward, watchful, taunting. But
it's to me he says,

'Long way down here, devil take it ... you know how
long. Very tired now. Eh, that's the way of it.' He's too
serious for what he says.

'That's the way of it!' sings someone else. 'Certainly! *Coo-
coo!*'

'Again you?' Vassili asks me. I nod yes. He says, 'That's
good.'

'I see you know Vassili!' a garlic voice laughs on my right,
spinning his finger around his ear and then around mine.
'Good fellow! Good *partisano!* Only a little –'

Peculiar. Yes, I guess he could be. I didn't really think
about it when I was up in the Pelikano, where everyone is
a little abrupt and strange, with the same noses and casts in
their eyes.

Over by the fire where four beheaded sheep are turning
slowly, butcher Socrati slits the air with his cleaver. 'Like that
... fix it right!' he's saying, and there's a ripple of laughter.

Holding still all over, Vassili rolls his bites from one cheek
to the other, pauses to listen and reaches long-armed for his
wine. Now up goes half a potato, hap! and the stumps of
his teeth tear it back and forth, his pupil-less blue eyes looking
out unconcernedly. He drives in some long green beans too,
chews, stops, chews, his fallen shoulders bent around his
plate. He eats with his whole body, his hands helping his arms
and his boots keeping time. Watching him, I understand how

he's lived up there by the sheer strength of himself since time began, and how he still might go on living.

'Fix him for good ... *tak-a-tak!* Then no more trouble! Hear, Vassili?'

'*Tak-a-tak*, he says!' P. Arkilaki nudges Vassili and nods to the butcher, who repeats the cutting gesture at the end of the table. Vassili straightens, chews, and shakes his head, not understanding.

Someone hears an engine coming. Everyone turns and looks. But it's only the generator at the stationhouse. The mood of the town isn't right.

'One day, they both come off!' says the butcher, and another peal of laughter follows.

I get up to leave.

'This way we go, and this way –' Grigori tips back Vassili's chair while he still sits calmly with his fork and his knife. Andreas dives for his two suspended boots.

'Stop!' Vassili shouts thickly as his chair rises and rocks obscenely in the air.

'I know what he does up there! Don't I know? With all those free hours, ey, slowly-slowly, he makes an army of little Vassilis up there in the mountains!' Butcher Socrati hurries up behind the line of wide black backs.

'Nothing I do!' Vassili bellows, uncoiling forwards.

'You do!' says Socrati, menacing the great shape with the blade. Pappa Steliano tries to restrain him and stop the joke, but he turns away himself with shaking shoulders.

'An army of Vassilis, I say! Now, *zeeti-zeet!* then everything's all right! No worries!'

Mercifully, Kristo's yellow lights bounce into view, and the chair is lowered. The general's riding in the sidecar. He bumps around in a circle and comes to a halt before the table.

And the dinner begins again. But every now and then as

Socrati turns the sheep he calls, 'Do you hear? I promise, one
day – '

Others gesture Vassili back to the table, but he won't
move. He sits on the porch and watches with folded arms,
and finally he goes away.

I stop in the heat of the field to see the long flights of herons
sweep safely in over the coast from Gavdos and Libya. The
mystery of travelling birds. They turn over the house, bank
and settle in long narrowing lines among the boulders by the
river where the gypsies were. When I walk along the mill
path, they spread their wings and hiss at my boots, dancing
out from nowhere on their long stick-legs, foreign, sinister,
too big and unafraid for here.

It's already spring. The sheep fill the roads with dust, starting up the first hills with the baaing of the new lambs and
the shepherds' whistles and shouts.

Now every Sunday morning at dawn Pappa Dimitri, the
mountain priest, closes his gate at the end of the town and
starts off with his dog to Maza and Rodovani on the track
through the sea shingle, toppling forwards under the weight
of his shotgun, his boots gliding quickly under his robe to
keep him from falling.

He goes into the cemetery for a moment and brings out
his white goat, who stands up to nibble the new mulberry
leaves hanging along the roadside. By the time Pappa Dimitri
reaches the spring by my house, he's bent double with the
strain of pulling her, coming along thoughtfully, holding the
rope behind him with both hands. Each time I see that odd
shape pitching forwards through the carob trees, I know
another week has passed.

'Come and we'll see how many priests we have up there
today,' the Pappa calls to me softly, with his white teeth
showing in his beard. He takes out his water bottle and stops

the drain in the stone trough with a ball of plane leaves. 'Poor soul, Vassili,' he says after a minute. 'But it won't do, that.'

Vassili has gone wild since that night in the town. He's living in the police station now, where they can watch him better. His hut up in Vassilaki has been pulled down. They've cropped his hair short like Crazy Panayoti's and taken away his shoes.

The morning after the military celebration, they say Vassili stopped the Vouta bus to tell everybody inside that Paleochora was full of snakes, and that people should stand up and fight while they still could. And each day after that, he stopped the bus and waved and shouted again that time was running short. It made the trips lighter for Stelio, the driver, and he always pulled over and opened the door to listen and argue with the wild man while the passengers got out to piss and shoot birds.

Then, two weeks ago, for no apparent reason, Vassili walked across the mountains to the church at Maza, put on Pappa Dimitri's gold and blue cassock and hid himself and the ikons in the catacombs at Azogeri.

'I don't know why,' the priest says under the blowing plane tree. 'I don't know what he was thinking of, trying to save the ikons for himself. Do you? Eh, that won't do, Yakovo, playing priest up there. And now I can't help him,' says Pappa Dimitri with a glance to one side. Like one of the Turk-gouged frescoes in his church, his brown eyes look down over his hollow cheeks and the straight, meeting lines of his nose and mouth. He stands there thinking a moment more, then he shakes his head and tugs his goat on up the road again with his old dog running ahead.

Vassili trudges around Paleochora as if he's always been there, following this one to the post office, that one to the

Government Monopolió shed. Like Crazy Panayoti, they
keep him busy in the town, useful, out of the way.

He walks behind Evangeli's rubbish cart, and he kicks olive
oil drums down the beach to the mill with his bare feet, a
sweat-band tied around his bristly bullet head. He helps unload the Herakles-Olympos boat at the pier, with his wild
eyes staring from his cement-powdered face. And sometimes
he stalks out past the carpenter's shop to the end of the asphalt
and stands alone looking at the mountains over the lane of
sighing eucalyptus trees.

But I usually see him in crowds of people – ducking behind
the heads gathered around a Chania businessman who has
come on the noon bus and spread his suitcase of popguns and
red feather dusters out on the street. Or I see him waving
straight-armed from a ring of poor Gavdos women pruning
olive trees, or hunched importantly over his candle in the
church.

Suddenly Vassili is everywhere, calling his garbled, high-
pitched greetings. He cuts over to the motionless figures on
the shady side of the street when the bottom of a chair is
slapped and spun around for him. And of course everyone
laughs and welcomes a change in the suspense and heat. A
new crazy man in town.

Singly, people are a little afraid of him. He shouts excitedly
and shakes his finger while the person he's talking to sits
obliterated and uncomfortable, looking away. Yet, together,
four or five voices call, 'Ya-su, Vas-si-li!' drawn out like a yell
across the canyon, with a duck-quack or a bird-call at the end.

I feel sorry whenever I see him, more than sorry. There's
always something familiar about him sitting by himself in
a kafenion or out on the fortress wall. I think of the time
I met him up in the Pelikano. It seems like a year has passed
since then. But it hasn't been a year, it hasn't even been two
months.

We talked together that day, then he walked one way and Katina and I went another, and afterwards nothing was left – no hut, no field of artichokes, neither of us even, exactly as we were. Sometimes I wonder if even the Pelikano valley is still up there under the rolling clouds.

One morning in April when I was cutting furrows for the summer field, Vassili strolled calmly out my kitchen door with a handful of pencils held out in front of him like a fan, and my typewriter tucked under his other arm.

'Here we are today again, father!' he called in a single burst. 'To the devil with the rest of the weasels, eh? What stuff! Well, goodbye! Nice work, we'll do!'

I picked up my cheese-and-olives lunch and my box of watermelon seeds and edged through a break in the bamboo fence just as he came down onto the road.

'Come, take these instead,' I said.

I held my things out to him, and he stopped reluctantly in the sunshine and scratched his chin.

'Seeds and food. All right!' he said. He shrugged and tipped his head. 'Poor soul! Can you show me the spring?'

We exchanged loads and started back to the spring along the shadow of the road trees. I put the pencils in my pocket and left my machine on the oven ledge.

'Wait! *Ap!* There's more!' Vassili found a little goat bell in the grass by the amphora and tossed it in the door.

From my window I watched him sitting against the green sea under the dome of the plane tree. He crossed one leg over the other, munched at the bread and gazed at the sky. I wrote in my notebook that the same amount of time had passed for both of us, that we'd shared these three months, and then – And then I lost the thought.

I straightened my papers with a tap and put two stray

books back on the shelf. I stared out at my hoe standing on end where I'd stopped in the middle of the field, and where the black turned soil stopped too.

The river is going low, and it's not even Easter yet. It could be another dry year.

At night I hear big feet splashing down the water ditch behind the house, then the spillway closes to a tinkling of voice-like drops. It makes me want to laugh, these secret thefts of my water so early in the year. It rushes away under the vineyard wall and down across the road, and soon the crickets begin to sing in P. Arkilaki's melon field. In the morning, Manoli lets the dry soil run through his fingers, and he curses Yanni and kicks at the air.

P. Arkilaki has spread a sheet of clear plastic on posts over his square of green in the beach boulders. Not a single water-melon was stolen or sun-scorched, and he sold an early crop at a wonderful profit. Now the riders on the road say, 'Po! Clever, that one!' and, 'Arkilaki knows what!'

He's planted again and added a comfortable board hut in a corner where he sits on a chair he carried out from town. As if drawn there, a visiting gunboat with a black number 28 rests on the glassy water above him, throbbing and turning slowly in the current a mile out from the pier.

Today Kristo gave Vassili ten drachmas to frighten the crows away from the road. He stops his motorcycle good-naturedly to discuss the work. Vassili listens, salutes and jerks himself about, repeating what he has to do.

'Yanni?' P. Arkilaki calls invisibly from his hut at the sounds of the shouts and crashing branches on the roadside. 'Yakovo? Who?' he calls through the still afternoon.

HOLY WEEK

MORE AND MORE PEOPLE ARE COMING FOR EASTER
week, bits of red and black switching down the hill paths.
Buses and lorries of relatives steer out of the canyon with
blue and white flags on the fenders and everyone standing
up in holiday clothes, singing mechanically in different
directions.

Morris and I ride down the back street. Grannies in black
pass us with their pans of parsley-covered pig meat to cook
at the bakery, hurrying around us to feed the gaiety in the
square. I look between the buildings at the droves of brightly
dressed women swelling back and forth in sunglasses and
pointed shoes, and the children rolling stiffly behind in chif-
fon and pink pressed felt. The brave Cretan men are ready
with their umbrellas and new Easter suits. There has to be
an Easter.

Kristo's motorcycle is back here out of sight, chained to
an oil drum in a ditch. I look over Manoli's blue gate as we
pass. He and Espasia are facing one another in chairs in the
sprinkled courtyard. A relative with a vest and Espasia's same
bulb nose sits between them clicking his beads smartly. I tip
my hat as I glide by, and they nod very slightly. Kristo play-
fully aims and snaps his Luger from the window.

Morris snorts and sighs when I tie him to the ring on the sagging bakery stairs. I've ridden him the whole way today, because, in Paleochora, no one walks on holidays. On holidays, people are finer than usual. 'Hot!' they call to you, or, 'Too far!' or just, 'Get on your donkey!' And even the clustered hens turn their yellow beaks as one to see who this gypsy is, tramping down their back street on a Saint's Day.

'Long life, Yakovo!' The Gavdos Manuso buttons himself and turns from the collapsed seawall at the end of the corridor, with his red-checked apron tucked under his arm.

'Many years, Manuso!' I take my bag off the saddle. 'Bread today?'

'Bah, with so many priests? The bread's slow,' he says. 'Wait a minute, not to get wet.'

High sea today. The waves are exploding on the fortress and breaking down to the hand-blackened bakery door. We run over the stones as the water seeps away under our boots again.

Inside, Pappa Dimitri is stamping the dough with his brass church seal, muttering, carefully passing each loaf to a red-bearded priest I've never seen before: 'And this one ... and another ready ... *yasu*, Yakovo ... Manuso, where were you? ... come, a little water now....'

The women wait crookedly in the gloom along the smoky ochre walls, coming forwards now and then to peer into the oven with the lantern. 'Not yet, aunt. Wait a little,' Manuso says quietly each time without looking up from the rocking bread tub.

We wait ten minutes. We wait half an hour. Morris begins to stamp and call outside. And still the solemn voices, the swishing robes and the knock-knocking of Manuso's tub. In the end I leave with no bread at all.

At Yorgi's I ask for a coffee and get a banana brandy and

two peanuts. A pale idiot boy presses his face flat against the window behind me, glad to be out this once for Easter. Another maroon and grey bus whines onto the sticky tar in the square, stops with a jerk and a backfire and backs around to face the mountains again, laying down a stream of watch-chains and waving hands. Everyone nods, pleased, 'Many people this year!' Yorgi brings me a second banana brandy for free. I stretch my legs out to another chair and look at the thin, retreating clouds over the canyon cliff. Remarkable, a whole year has passed. Here we all are again, elbow to elbow, celebrating the loss of another time.

The sea-line bunches the houses together like white beads. The island comes to an end in Paleochora and piles up in a panic before the water. A little east wind is blowing the sea up in peaks. In the church tonight, they'll have to sing louder over the waves. Maybe that's why Greeks sing the way they do.

An obese city man, sleepy and red as a tomato, stops in the street before me with his mouth open. If you're fat, you're rich. I wipe my forehead with my sleeve. I've become too morose for holidays. I'm going to take a long walk with Morris and some sandwiches and come back after Easter.

His bulging city wife holds his arm high by the shoulder to show him better, and she calls through her nose to a window above, 'Kyria Eleni? Ah-hahaha! We're fine, don't you see? Thank you, yes! And the children? Lovely!–'

The husband looks at my muddy boots and I look at his yellow shoes, and he looks at his yellow shoes and I look at my muddy boots. He wipes his with a yard-square handkerchief, and I make a stack of mine. He frowns at the space of me with hooded eyes, rubbing his long fingernails together. The world is becoming the same, and the same is wrong. We're all piled up before the sea.

Holy Week. I pay Yorgi and lift up my knapsack to go home. I head Morris along the beach to miss the hired mourners on the cemetery road.

But when I get to the river I stop and realize, 'I'm not going home, I'm going to the mountains for Easter, and maybe I'll stay up there. Kristo could take me.'

Great Monday

'I don't understand you. Why do you want to spend The Week with sheep thieves? And why have you brought all these things? My taxi, now, maybe kaput from the road – No good, friend – Yakovo!'

Kristo pushed my baskets and roped box out of the sidecar and flicked his fingers hopelessly. Then he sped off in a rage, looping down into the warm green spring of Souya valley again. That was yesterday.

It seemed a pure thing to do, to come up to Maza, hidden high in the boulders and crags at the edge of the tundra. Kristo thought I should come on Holy Saturday, or even on Easter morning, not to have a long time in such a place. Espasia's relative agreed. But it seemed important to spend the whole Week in a village where Easter is still a personal event.

Fig Tuesday

The mayor met me with a knife and a severed sheep's head in his hands. He was a giant of a man with hobnailed boots and a black headcloth. His name was Apostolo.

'It's good you've come! Stay as long as you like!' he shouted, giving my beard a pull. 'One week! Two weeks! What news? Greetings, none?'

I actually had something – a grudging note from Kristo, crammed into a cigarette box:

> *Kristo Loupasis, son of*
> *Manoli, sends greetings*
> *from his family, who are*
> *well. Please take care*
> *of Mr Yakovo, a tourist.*

Apostolo took me to Widow Margarita. She lived alone at the top of the town in a house like a beehive, with one black eye peeping around the corner of the church. She scuttled out in new mourning clothes, cried and held my hands. She wanted to have me, it was no trouble at all. She showed me to a bare room upstairs – I could make a bed of logs and window shutters, and there was a helmet in the corner for the night.

Apostolo said Margarita's son hung himself from a fig tree two weeks ago. Nobody knew why. He spun his finger around his ear and said the boy was a little, eh! – and the mother was too. I said maybe another house would be better, then? But Apostolo was the mayor, and he said there wasn't one.

The boy was twenty-two. Zacharias. Margarita showed me a picture of him in the army, standing straight with a twisted face. Now she hears me in his old room and taps up and down the stairs bringing lamps and daisy tea, sweeping, singing, staring at my hands.

She throws a load of twigs on the fire and the flames fly up with a roar. We sit on the bench and watch the crackling olive branches, while she tells me how, on this same day, Christ cursed the barren fig tree for its answer to God.

Big thundering wind tonight, like waves on the coast. The moon has a halo high in the clear, cold air.

Oil Wednesday

This morning the room is filled with grannies perching on the bench and the step like wild black birds, whispering behind their hands. Margarita goes around with plates of almonds and red eggs. Our eyes meet and we all nod and smile, but who can be happy today? Apostolo has accused Margarita of selling the jugs of church oil. It happened an hour ago in the square where everyone could hear.

'Help, God! Where do we go?' moans a voice.

'The world is breaking,' says someone else in the dark.

'Whose oil is it, his? Hm!' Margarita folds her arms and wags her head. 'This won't do, my friends. I'll call the police! Then we'll find out how many sheep the cuckold has up there on the plateau! Don't we all know about that shit-bad man?'

'Peace, where is it?'

'If you're poor, you're blamed. Hm! Who got the blame the day the wise one came over the mountains and turned the church upside-down?'

'Hear! We're being eaten!'

It's too cold to sit in one place – I spend the day outside. The weather holds hard and bright, with many gladioli still left in the terraces and pink asphodels dancing tall along the walls. The children follow me in a crowd, showing me caves,

telling stories, singing our names together. Today we walk
to a rock-closed gully they call The Pot. They say a horse
with a horn on its head lived here once. People used to come
to catch him with a rope, but he just laughed and kicked and
ran in circles to show how free he was. Apostolo hit him with
a stone one day, and he galloped away.

Tonight the village turns red in the window, dims and disappears. Margarita pokes the coals and the sparks fly out in
ribbons, catching on the sifters and courtyard tubs.

'I told him, "Zacharias. Take the jugs with you to Chania.
Do whatever you understand. God helps us." Otherwise,
what hat would he have? Even sheep have shoes.'

Judgement Thursday

It's almost May, and it's snowing. That's the risk, going to
a high place. Strong, grey day, with the wind pouring past
the paneless window in a roar. I've never seen it snow in
Greece before.

'Hurry! Get up! It's the Judgement!' Margarita's pounding the floor with a broomstick and fitting her big eye to
a knothole. 'Tea, I have, and cheese! What are you doing
up there? Just burning my wood?'

I find her in the kitchen, muttering and shaking her head,
wrapped in a blanket with her hair in a tangle. She's hearing
voices in the smoky rafters again, she remembers how they
cut her Zacharias down and stretched him out in the room
upstairs. He'd hung himself from the top of the tree where
no one would see his boots. It was a snowy morning, like
today. He was sitting here in his overcoat, picking sesame
seeds out of his bread one at a time. She asked him where
he was going, and he kissed her and said, 'Up above, to find
the sheep. Give me the rope.'

'Ask everyone what I did and how I was,' Margarita says
over her shoulder, lying down on the floor. 'I went from

house to house asking how my Zacharias could die. Who decides? Do you know? Tell me!'

She's painted a white cross over the doors and the court-yard gate because this is the night we must see Christ. We'll hear Judas first, clapping outside by the well and calling us to follow him. But we'll be still, not a word at all. Then Christ will come like a brightening star and nothing we ever knew will be like Him.

Good Friday

Children come asking for old clothes for the effigy. Apostolo's nailed a cross of cedar and barrel-bands: tonight, they're going to catch Judas and put him up instead of our Lord. They'll cover him with lamp oil, there being no other, and set him on fire Easter morning. People are all for burning him right now, after what he's done. No one fails to pass the stuffed, leering shape of Judas without throwing a stone and a curse.

Two more days until Easter.

Kristo has called from Paleochora. They came to the house to tell me, and we ran through the rain to the crank-telephone in Apostolo's house. Kristo talked of passing near here on business tonight and said he could still bring me down home in time for the Event. In fact, it seemed rather definite. Useless to explain that the liturgy was in a matter of hours. He said he'd only come to ask me: I could go or stay, just as I liked. I thanked him, but I *willed* him not to come. When I got back, Margarita was asleep on the kitchen floor: only snores and the bottoms of her feet coming out the door.

Early in the night I dream I'm down at the house and the fields are hot and full of melons. The sea is green and still, and Gavdos floats closer across the water, covered with shrines and bending palm trees. Margarita comes calling down the road with a sack of food from Maza. I look inside and there are figs and cheese stuck together with a pink paste, and underneath them is a tiny wide-eyed fish. Then I find a grey, whole liver, and when I pull it out I see that a lamb has been slaughtered over the top. Margarita spreads a cloth in the shade by the spring and sets three places. Kristo watches the whole thing from the roadbank, and then he sputters away on his motorcycle with a cloud of spiraling dust.

Big Saturday

The bells in Souya have rung all day. That's where Pappa Dimitri is. If he were here, our bells would be ringing too. They say he'll come up late tonight, after the services in Moni and Livadia.

The chapel is scrubbed clean, with its candleholders polished and all the brass basins filled. The tired old saints on the walls bend down and scowl every time a whistle-bomb goes off in the churchyard. Tension hangs over the mountainside because time is passing and Christ is still in Purgatory.

In the evening I hear a flock of goats being driven into town with shouts and crashing rocks, and then the streets are covered with blood. More and more little tied shapes lying in the square for the feast, screaming like hysterical children. Then the blood is on the tree trunks and boulders and dripping down the steps.

Great gales come one after the other, with the house creaking like a ship and the roof trying to fly off. A shutter rips away downstairs and the board floor parts with a hiss. I hear Margarita struggling and holding onto things in the wild, dark night.

Easter: The Event

The bells start at midnight. Margarita bumbles upstairs and leaves a candle for me. 'Stand! Take this! It's now!'

The wind's down, the stars are out – who has ever known so many? Everyone has a light: candles, torches, little *liknos* lamps with wicks of twisted cotton, all winding up the paths to the chapel and coming together there. Judas is nailed to the cross, leaning out from the churchyard wall with a fez cap and a confident grin, sort of asking for it, with his potato-nose and his eight old shoes tied on. We put our lights on the long wall. We can hear the bells across the valley. I wonder if they can hear ours, piping over the cliff and down through the olive trees.

Everyone's here, now where is the Pappas? Apostolo says he's breaking the fast, probably stuffing himself down there in Souya. But after a while there's the rasping sound of a motorbike circling up in the dark. A headlight bounces into view – it's Corporal Lazaro of the Mountain Police and the Pappas is hanging on behind, waving the news: '*Kristos anesti!* Christ is risen!'

We light little tapers from his ikon lamp and follow him inside past the bier of flowers and the shining bowls, with the bell tolling madly the whole time and shotguns roaring outside. Someone lights Judas too early, and he starts to moan and move his arms in the billows of oily smoke. But he won't burn because his rags are too damp and old – and who has the money to throw paraffin on him this year? I can see him laughing in the window, more or less intact, only someone's thrown mud in his face and knocked off his hat.

'*Kyrie eleison!*' Pappa Dimitri will cut the talking short because of the late hour and all the smoke. We're happy and we cheer and shake hands, while Margarita flicks cologne and pelts people with daisies. The donkeys call over their shoulders at the popping firecrackers and all the shouting, and the children are running and beating on pans, even drowning out Corporal Lazaro's '*Long Live the Greek Ethnic State!*'

Margarita laughs and cries and gives me two cold kisses.
'Christ is up! Think what it means!'

The morning dawned pure and fresh for the long walk home,
with the village doves flying and the smell of woodsmoke
and thyme in the air. Their feast would be soon. I could hear
a fiddle tuning up.

Margarita wouldn't take any money, but I hid some for
her anyway, which she found and expected. She filled my
knapsack with daisy tea and brown bread and walked as far
as the graveyard with an apronful of asphodels for Zacharias:

'When you get to where you're going, tell them greetings
from Mirizakis, Margarita, widow of Kariotis, whose only
son God took.'

TO GAVDOS

THE LIGHT LEAVES THE LAND UNTIL ONLY THE GULLS
are diving on low between the waves – and the half-moon,
holding the sombre fact of itself upside-down. Riding home
in the evening, I wonder at the May red clouds parting and
dissolving over the frontier of Gavdos. More fantastic plumes
and towers loom beyond them, cloud-worlds, deeper and
wilder still.

Turkey is somewhere under there, plains of grass sweeping
back without plan or meaning from the neat little sea-world
of Greece. The colours must be old and restful there, brown
and gold and dark green. Life must be close to a dream in
space like that, never seen or heard of again, with all its
longings gone.

It must take one strong push away to leave the dying,
familiar place I'm in. Then I'll drift on quite easily again.
Only the leaving was hard, I'll say afterwards.

Yet as I unpack the saddle bag and light the lantern on the
table, the peace of the night-kitchen begins again, the sluiceway bubbling by outside, the exercise book laid out willingly
with a pencil in it, Sofia purring invisibly. I pour a red wine
and think, 'After the week in Maza,' where else would I be
but here?'

Nevertheless, an hour later I hurry back down the beach again. It's Saturday evening, boat-evening. I'm leaving for Gavdos tonight. I'm just going to do it, I'm not going to think. I run, walk, run again with the spoons and a tin plate banging in my knapsack. I have the blue-ribbed basket on my arm and Sofia's in it. One of her big, dependent kittens darts through the brush at the side and warbles his tomcat call behind us when I wade across the river into the bamboo.

'Why?' Kristo asks tediously when we meet in town. But Manoli just smiles, always separate. He has his hoe and two lemon seedlings – he's just closing his gate to go out to the grove. All he says is, 'Go well, then.' I ask him to take care of the animals again, and he laughs yes self-consciously and fidgets his vest on and off. I will or won't come back, he can't tell.

Sofia stares from under the basket lid as we wait at the end of the pier. Captain Sava looks tired and old, sitting by himself beside the water tap in the square with his nets strung across the post office like a spider web. He's taking a priest out to Gavdos tonight, probably the red-beard I saw in the bakery a while ago. On Gavdos, Easter is this week. Do I know why?

Sava shuffles wearily out towards us in his baggy clothes and readies his cooker and his ikon light. We still have to wait for the priest. Sava smokes a cigarette and coils his nets on a canvas. It's dark, the lights are already in the windows, but there's still no Pappas. So Captain Sava starts the motor with a yank and says, 'Let him swim.'

No one talks much about Gavdos. People are sorry it's there; especially forward men like Manuso who have made it in Paleochora and are ready for another jump north. Niko the postman sends Wise Vassili down to the pier with the empty mail sack every Saturday to avoid meeting needy relatives. Streetsweeper Evangeli no longer remembers exactly where he was born. 'Down there,' he says crossly with a wave towards Libya. Even on maps, Crete is a better, more shapely end to Greece and Europe.

Soon the town looks like a crowd of purple sails on the horizon. Is it possible to be going further south? A little sparrow flies up sleepily from the deck, wheels around in a fright and settles on the mast again. Even as we watch, the low peninsula and the cliff fall into the darkness. The warm yellow lights of Maza begin to twinkle above, between the marching Orion and the bright eye of Sirius risen on the eastern mountains.

Then for the first time, it's gone – the embers of Crete bend back strangely and curve down under the starry sky. How small it was – finished! Something rises in me and looks ahead.

Sava sits on the cabin step with his beaked army cap turned up. He's lashed the wheel to a peg in the roof, and his fish dinner is boiling. Hours pass and we just sit looking. Soon the mound of Gavdopoula islet appears in the starlight ahead. Sava makes a cutting motion halfway up his arm. The skiff streaks unreally through the dark behind us, the only mark on the gently heaving water. We sit still until the first great distance has passed.

Sava likes to talk about the war over the hammering of his motor. I ask him which one, because there are half a dozen, just now. I could see the flashes of the one in Egypt at night sometimes from the oven ledge.

'In Albania!' he says, surprised. 'What other?' He makes a fist. 'Cold there? Po! Mules, Yakovo, frozen like this. . . .'

I find I don't really want to hear him. I'm glad there's more than what Sava knows.

I wake up later knowing we're very far out. It's dawn and we're still moving. I pull back the canvas blanket and blink into the first light. Sofia's looking too, riding up and down on the roof of the wheelhouse. The sound of the motor is coming back to us across a sheet of still water. Sava says, 'Must wait a bit ... to see well.'

When the motor shuts off, I hear sea birds and the faint wash of waves. There's something in the greyness – a trough of boulders coming down into the water, and straight above there's a line drawn across the sky. The western cliffs – but *huge*, pitted, overhanging, still advancing in the pink glow.

A breeze brings the land-heat across. When I stand up, I look down the full reach of Gavdos, enlarged a hundred times from the hazy, flat shape I saw from the house, drawn forward with unexpected crescent coves and gullies full of scrub cedars, cut in the centre by a deep lightless cleft. There are *miles* between the first bare hills and the white chalk backbone, uncoiling down from the cliffs to the low eastern tip. Beyond, open water again.

A figure in a robe or a skirt bounds up onto the rocks of the nearer skyline, watches a moment, then dashes back out of sight. The boat crawls around the head of a hidden bay towards a landing and a roofless house. A few dead-looking buildings appear on a treeless rise above, just an abruptness of rectangles put out on the hottest possible place. The only sign of life is still the one lone shape striding wildly alongside, keeping up, free-falling down the powdery hillside before us with a rifle on his back and a black dog dropping behind him.

The anchor drops. I tie my cloth-covered basket and stand ready to go. A tip of the sun shows. But Sava just uncovers his nets. He's not going ashore yet.

Why? Who knows? He closes his eyes and waves all my questions away, stalking back and forth from his bait-box to the wheelhouse. And he's in a rage about something.

I look from the turning bow to the man waiting by
the water with his slumped shoulders and his arms at his
sides.

'Ey – ?' Sava straightens and opens his hands, showing me
his self-evident work. 'Take the little boat in,' he says. 'It
doesn't matter to me!'

So I pull the oarless skiff alongside hand over hand, and
lower Sofia over the gulf of water with a screech. I push off
hard towards the flat-rock landing, where the man squats on
his heels and watches me with field glasses.

'All right, and then what do I do with the rowboat?' I call
back.

'Boat?' says Sava, busy.

'How do you get the boat back?'

'*Who?* Who gets the boat?' he shouts, flinging his jumbled
net down. 'Whatever you understand: do it!'

I make a wave to the squatter, who wears a white cloth
wrapped around his head with just a slit left for his eyes, and
a sun-faded green coat tied around his waist by the sleeves.
I nod to him as I glide in. I coil the skiff rope and put a stone
on the coil. But now that I'm here, he won't look up. '*Erba!*'
he calls instead in a falsetto and rolls his dog over on its back,
lifting his head as if to strike it. '*Erba!*' The silly beast yaps
and winces and rolls its eyes. I make for the shade of the fallen
house.

Sava's still bent over his buckets and hooks in the flashing
water behind. The new heat is confusing.

'Should we go on to the village?' I call from the shadow.
I can't seem to begin the experience of being here.

But this stunned man wags his head, neither yes nor no.
No answer. So I glance up and take a grip on the basket.
I will go to the village, and then things will start.

'Now,' he says to me, rising and calling back, '*Eh! Sava,
yásu!*'

'Meester Georgie!' Sava flings up a hand without turning from all his fishing.

'Are you from here?' I ask Mr Georgie. 'From Gavdos?' Because his stride shows he's not, his split shoes lifting up the ash-like dust and bowling back the blotches of thyme.

He stops wide-eyed and fumbles a sleeve of his coat around to show me two dull police chevrons. Who could be from Gavdos? Who? We wait in the sun in the middle of the hillside until I've said, 'No one.'

'No one! Certainly!' he says, plunging on. 'Bad place, my friend! How many people are here? How many, do you think?'

I say, 'Maybe two hundred.'

'Sixty,' he snorts. 'That's company?'

Mr Georgie has been on Gavdos for two years. He's Cretan, from Chania, at first. Then he admits to Theriso, the Venizelos town, and finally to tiny Kyriakosellia, a roadless stack of houses in a gulch further south. On Crete, it's a matter of pride, where you're from.

The houses disappear over the ridge. We watch them go. Mr Georgie says the place is called Vatsiana. It's evidently deserted, but Mr Georgie says no. At mid-morning a second village, Kastri, is dancing above us in the heat. The double-ringed sun comes down closer, and the sky turns white. It seems a wonder, being here. Hedgehogless sort of a place.

For a while the trail winds along a dry river bed covered with burrs, then it turns and charges blindly at one of the hillocks of white loam, drives up over it in a straight line, dropping down again at an angle, always in towards the swell of the big ridge. Up and down, around, up again, and nothing is ever said. There's just the squeaking of Mr Georgie's battered street shoes and the pale blur of heat.

Finally the path runs against the ridge rocks and explodes into hundreds of rabbit tracks, all downwards, in all directions. Kastri is right below, built on a smooth sheet of rock without a tree or a shadow, fifteen or twenty stone houses piled along the rim of the gorge, turning as the gorge turns. From up here the drop only seems like a shift of the earth, there's no idea how deep it is. The inlaid path and two ruined windmills on the far side are slightly lighter and lower than the mosaic of square roofs and windowless walls, and the sea-gulls plane down and suddenly vanish between there and here.

The paths still run on out of sight – one wandering off to the white mote of a chapel on the headland, one to the east towards the long bars of Vatsiana, another to a little, distant tree, and another winding down the crest of the ridge, worn right into it. Everywhere, the longer I look, I see the faint network of trails and near-invisible ruins. The solitude of the island spreads until it is complete.

We're so low in the the sky. Are the valleys safe? The sea sweeps around in a circle almost overhead, the quarter-moon of Gavdopoula drifting even with us through the dark blue stillness. Everything in the immense silence is drawn to the one little patch of Kastri – and Mr Georgie far ahead, running down to it across the shingle-covered fields.

Two men shuffle down the slate street. Another cuts one-mindedly across their path, and the three of them disappear together into a black, signless door.

'Mail: nothing! ... no priest ...,' Mr Georgie is saying when I lean in. In the darkness I trace two bare feet back to a shape lying on a cot. Then I make out a neck, a cloth hat and four sets of folded arms. The room is lined with white faces and hands on the benches around the walls.

'This one here knows my town, knows Crete!' says Mr Georgie, pacing back and forth under a shelf of tins. It's a kind of coffeehouse-store. 'Tell them about my town, friend, tell them! Bravo!'

There's a silence.

'It's a white town ... shady from plane trees ...,' I say.
'The houses have deep wells....'

'What are you saying!' someone whispers.

'Listen!' Mr Georgie giggles insanely. 'Hear! A white
town! White! Clean! And water for each house!'

'Snow, it has, in the winter ... very cold....'

'Cold, hear, God.'

'Miracles! Hoo, there you live!' says Mr Georgie.

'And cattle?' The boots slide on the floor and the benches
creak.

'Cattle! Everywhere cattle and flowers!' says Mr Georgie.

'If there are cattle, then of course there are horses and
geese,' says the body on the cot.

'A happiness,' another old voice calls.

'Come, Kouma! Enough! Get up! He's staying, the
foreigner. Hee! Hee!' Mr Georgie goes to the door and back
again, whistling and snapping his fingers. 'He wants to live
in that old house of yours. I know what he wants.'

The corpse rises slowly and strains forward on another's
shoulders to reach a key on the wall.

'And take this too,' Mr Georgie snatches up a lantern without a globe.

'Take it, take everything,' someone says hopelessly in the
dark.

'Bad people, eh?' Mr Georgie elbows me and laughs when
we're out in the white heat again. 'Bad, a little. Eh?' he asks,
watching me so closely that he stumbles on a stone and
throws out his arms to catch himself. 'Did you see how
stupid? Never mind, a few more years, and who'll be here?'

We climb back to the last house on the hill. It's set in a
deep courtyard with a dead arbour, the wall continuing out
into the great light and ending in a clump of prickly pears.
It's an edgeless sort of house, old and pretty inside, with queer
bulging windows and a funnel of a fireplace in the corner

with pots and a long-handled spoon hanging on it. Smooth blue-washed walls, like cave walls, flow down from the timbered ceiling. The shapeless chairs, the bed and the heavy table are low to the ground, as if made for children. Sofia climbs the rickety stairs ahead of me and stands still in an empty room with one tiny arched door open on the mud roof.

I cover the cupboard shelf with some of my writing paper and arrange the bits of food I brought. I hang the basket on a hook. I open the shutters and look out over the stubbly field at a ruined red-rock outbuilding with a swastika over the door and a scrawl of barbed wire around it. Sava's boat is still bobbing above the cactus and the white hills.

'Husband's dead! War! *Dan-dan!*' As he leaves, Mr Georgie points to a grey-hooded woman who bows and says she's from the house down the path. She lights the ikon lamp in a wall niche and then sits on the bench outside with her shawl caught between her teeth. A ragged little girl comes out of her skirts and stands with her back to me. The widow tells her in a whisper everything she sees.

Sofia says she has nothing to do. She puts her feet up on the wall and alternately mews to herself and bothers the widow. But I'm busy filling my new shelf. I like getting ready for the first evening.

I walk around the house outside, seeing things one at a time. I peer into the row of amphoras by the stable door and check the empty shed behind, where I find a *Gott Mit Uns* belt buckle, like a tiny weight on a haystack. The slope of the stony field has gone wrong, I notice. I could grow things here, but only just. The widow's head follows me right and left, up and down. She doesn't want to talk. Which is fine.

It's already growing dark in the corners of the courtyard – the shadows feel around the oven canopy and across the garden of hard white clods. I'm standing at the nailed board gate looking down the path when three men with a cedar-branch stretcher turn into view and start up the hill. The doors shut softly all along the street ahead of them. Someone is dead.

'The shopkeeper here likes his paraffin better than his ouzo!' Mr Georgie calls in, stalking along at the side of the bearers with a stick.

'Same colour, bad luck ... couldn't smell it....' A withered hand lifts in greeting from the stretcher.

An hour later when the women and donkeys are coming back down the paths to town, I see the red speck of the boat far, far out to sea with a sick man aboard and nowhere to go.

At dawn the women trot away under the wall with their scythes and stick-rakes. It could be something glad, the little donkeys running away under them into the morning. But the cloaked shapes sit tired and still with downcast faces, their feet bouncing lifelessly over the whir of eager steps.

Mr Georgie has his shirt off behind the stationhouse, lifting weights in time with the crackling Arab music from his radio on the wall.

The widow leads her goat onto her roof, shades her eyes and sees me on mine.

Then the molten sun rides up on the ridge, and the blue shadows vanish from the feet of the hills. The sunlight curls around the well in the square and touches the cobblestones and closed doors. The pile of houses begins to lengthen and fuse in the heat, jumping like pistons. There's not a sound or a breath of wind.

The widow carefully closes my gate and slides into her morning place on the bench with her same hard smile. 'Stand!' she hisses to the girl when I come out for the day.

And there's the widow looking out vacantly from her burlap hood, her bobbin dancing low on the courtyard stones. 'Hot,' she whines, and the girl squeaks, 'Good morning.'

They won't have tea, not if it's my tea. A brightness comes into the widow's eyes, and she makes a slow upward nod: no.

'Fa! *See* how he eats! *See* the lovely things!' she says to the girl, turning her bird-shoulders around with her hands. I offer my plate, but up goes the nod again with a click of the tongue. 'Ap!–' she says when I bite my bread.

'And no more food now –' she sighs with her voice trailing up. She sets the bobbin going again, forcing me to watch it.

'No food?'

'Ha?'

'No food?'

'Ey, *nein*. He closed his store, Kouma, the sick one.' She turns an imaginary key in the air. 'Closed! *Klak!*'

'And in Vatsiana, nothing?'

'Do I know anything about it? I'm poor. I'm not the only one. Vatsiana comes here. Eat the cat!'

'Now, what does all that mean?' I wonder. 'You'll have to ask about that today. More than ask!' I say to myself.

I hum and push a piece of candy closer to the girl along the bench. She shifts from one pencil-leg to the other, breathing hard, crossing her toes.

I make the candy jump over the cobwebby grapevine and then I sit by it, leaving a little room. She stands still, she looks at the gate with her head on her shoulder and brown hands squirming.

I give her my present stiffly with my arm out straight: 'Take it, *para 'to.*' It touches her open palm and she swallows. The widow spins her bobbin again, cackling, immovable.

'*Mama,*' sobs the girl without moving. Her fingers won't

close on it. '*Mama*. I don't want it.' Her face is twisted, she's going to cry if I touch her again.

'The sweets – she doesn't like them,' the widow laughs. 'Ey – children!'

Sofia puts her feet up on the wall and looks at us all upside-down.

These minutiae are interesting to me, since I may come here to live.

The quietest step in the valleys frightens up flocks of sea ravens who have come scavenging inland, right under the boulders and trees. What does it mean, the big black birds hunting in so far? They beat up in blizzards from the branches around me, lashing out from the shadows of the dry river. Then there's nothing but the lizards rustling deep under the rocks. All the island is waiting, waiting for something, with only the soft rushing of waves beyond the dune-covered cedars.

I pass house after house between the loose, bleached hills. A heavy loom with dolphins carved on it stands out in the open: another bullet-riddled place, filled with timbers crossing down in the noon sun. A scorpion scuttles under a broken cup on the table.

And here's a closed door by itself, weathered grey, wired shut. I walk all around the walls, but the stoned-up windows tell me nothing about it. The house and its sandy field are at the very end of this valley – not even a valley, but a scree-filled hollow now. I try to picture a life here, and the quiet years of seasons around it. But it seems too late. The land is making some new condition. On the far side, in the shadow of the hill, there's still a trickle of water in a shell-mortar sluice-way leading to nowhere. A cloud of red and yellow hornets follow the water down the hillside to where it stops in a tuft of green grass. Someone has closed the spillways with flat rocks a long time ago, and now the bright little stream ebbs straight away through the heat – such a tiny sound, hardly there at all, stopping sometimes, almost lost.

I start up to the white chapel on the headland through fields crossed with forgotten boundary walls. Inside, the gloomy vault is alive with frescoes and lights from the sea: angels are leading a procession of armoured knights to a city of blue-and-gold-striped towers. Behind them come the damned, chained together by a crimson snake. And over the open door there is a tiny, winking man like a monkey. Then only the last, long buildings of Vatsiana, set apart like warehouses, lying dead on the ridge over the valleys I've been in.

When I stand outside in the shade of the fluted tiles, all at once I feel tired and broken to bits, as if I've come to a same beginning, or to the edge of a great drop. I want to wait a moment longer, hidden here, until I know what it is. Yet what if I were caught forever in an hour of time and there were no more changes in this surface-life but the black birds flying and the lines of the sea washing in? I feel something breaking inside me, coming free and turning away to save itself.

Today is Easter. That makes two this year. A spray of powdery dust streams off the courtyard wall. The gate creaks on its wooden hinges.

Today is Easter again, and a hot south wind is thundering down from the ridge. Sheets of water are blowing over the eastern end of Gavdos. The sea is churning back white as far as I can see. We're high under the shelter of the ridge rocks, but now and then a roar comes down the gorge without a trace and the air goes dim with silt. There is nothing left here to answer the sirocco. Just a heaviness of infinite days brought up in the air, finished, stifling. The houses in the doorway shudder blindly on the bare rock.

I put all the food I have on the table and feel along the shelf. 'Not enough,' I say. 'Well, then it's not.'

The skin is tight on my face. Each movement is so hopeless and small, and this irritates me. A breeze stirs the dust on the windowsill, then another hot breath comes over my hands. There's nowhere to go, no protection from the inescapable sky. My reach out from Crete is a room with Sofia and me sitting too close together at a crooked table.

I walk over to the widow's to ask her for her donkey. I will go up to the Easter in Vatsiana and eat. Things will be better when I'm moving outside.

The girl is on the step talking agreeably to herself and combing her hair with her fingers. She goes limp when she sees me. '*Ma-ma.*'

Two stump-feet stir on the straw inside. '*Ma-maa.*'

The widow fills the door. She smiles her queer smile at me standing on the path in the wind – at me coming to her for anything at all. But she isn't awake yet and her round face falls blank again. 'Donkey?' she says hoarsely, yawning and scratching her burlap stomach. 'What donkey?'

'Your animal eating grass there by the wall,' I say. Her donkey turns its loose white mouth around and chews, listening.

The widow shakes her head to wake up more and leans out, looking past me to see whether any more strangers are coming, or if it's just me waiting in the sun in her henscratched yard. 'Where will you go?' she spins her hand. '*Wo geht's?*'

'To Vatsiana. To the holiday.'

The widow slips back inside, as if with an idea, but she only reappears with her bobbin and her grey-brown yarn, her puff of wool bushed under her arm. She looks up the

path one more time, but there are still just the two of us.
Then she parts her lips over her teeth and slowly clicks her
tongue, no: ugly, prolonged, insulting.

I've just returned. I decided to walk there, down the trail into
the gorge, up through a notch in the ridge and off between
the windmills to Vatsiana.

A line of braying donkeys was tethered in the cover of the
first building, and the sound of a lyra with bells wavered up
between the slams of the wind. Nothing moved but a well
bucket wheeling over-end from its spindle, and the yellow
chaff billowing out from the threshingfloors.

Easter was in the kafenion. No food there either. The
widow knew.

'Look! Here he comes now, the priest! My saints, it's
Christ Himself!' said a skeleton at the door, pointing my
beard between his fingers and drawing it out like a horn.
Still, I smiled and gestured to a space on their bench for
myself. I took a glass of wine but explained that I couldn't stay
long.

The thin man, called Agroti, took an enormous straw-
bound bottle down the line of people standing along the
walls. No priest: no service. Everybody crossed himself and
held up his cup with a 'Kristos anesti!' No old people in the
room, I noticed. The lyra player sat drunk with his bell-
covered bow on his knee. Mr Georgie leaned sullenly in a
corner, not looking at anybody.

There was a terrific burst of wind, rumbling and droning
on all sides of the scene, and the door strained in on the bolt.
In the middle of the falling dust the lyra picked up again with
a rhythmic shaking of bells, and a man with one big eye and
one little one began to move in the centre of the dipping
floor. He looked up with a gulp and began to sing, and a

few others joined in over the gale. The whole time, the children pushed a board with a painted face around the floor. It careered into boots and bench legs, never wincing, no expression, backing up with a whistle and sliding on again with all of them stumbling behind it.

The straw bottle went around time after time, a bubbly red wine with sour fruit in it, possibly the grapes themselves. I didn't mind it. I had some more, and more again. A woman with a moustache and two others with close black eyes, sisters maybe, suddenly covered their mouths and giggled at me. People began to talk again. At some signal of his own, an enormous pig walked in from another room and looked about him with a grunt. I missed Katina. I wondered how Morris was getting along.

Agroti sat down next to me with two more full glasses. He apologized for the bad Easter: it was small, it was poor – *Yi*. He nodded to two turkeys who looked out from a blanket nailed to a table top. I turned my attention to the drama of them.

The hen turkey dashed towards the closed door, but the other one made a long jump before her, walking calmly again with a snap and a rustle of his feathers. She turned back to the blanket, but the billy-turkey puffed out his red and blue neck and snapped himself in front of her there too. She sighed and pecked at a crumb between my boots, and then the billy was on her, flopping and gobbling and digging with his spurs: all of it acutely uncomfortable to watch, being too much like people. Agroti elbowed me when I was drinking, and he laughed and stamped his feet.

Hours went by and the wind moaned stronger, so that the music and gobbles grew faint and far away. A shout or a thudding boot brought things back into focus for a moment, then slowly the view would sink and fade again, going, lost under the roaring outside.

I remember someone waving a revolver, cocking the hammer with both thumbs and firing into the ceiling with a grimace. There were screams around him and a single laugh. But the noise was too loud. It swept the room away and in the silence afterwards the wind rushed in.

I was endlessly sick while Mr Georgie was talking about Sava and the pier. Someone next to me picked up the pig's back legs, as if dancing with a baby, and the widow began to call from somewhere outside.

Mr Georgie has come back to the house with two eggs, two little brown eggs in his hand. 'That's it!' he laughs madly. 'No more!'

'What day is it?' I ask from the table. Bored Sofia creeps up and bites my pencil, then she yawns and looks out the glaring door.

'*Dienstag*, Thursday,' the widow helps from the courtyard.

Mr Georgie is silent for a moment, blinking, then he says, 'Two days more before the boat comes, bad luck.'

The sun moves away from the cupboard and the fireplace. The room is quiet, the mirror gleaming emptily on the wall as though I've already left.

I've gone down to the landing to wait for Sava to come from Crete. It's hot and still, not the slightest breeze. No sound but the monotonous waves.

Unbelievable heat. There's nothing on the coast but sun. We sleep until late in the afternoon in a pool of shade under a cedar. Nothing to do but wait and imagine eating.

Sofia lies awake, all pinched and crooked, all elbows and

ribs. She looks up through the branches with her paws over her ears. I wonder what she's thinking.

Mr Georgie appears this morning, coming leglessly down the coast through the mirage, shimmering out of sight, merging again out on the water, swinging his arms. His dog dives up and down beside him, floating over the dunes like a kite.

He waves and makes a long call, but when he drops down by me in the shade he only sits looking at the ground with his knees drawn in to him. No news. He's brought a loaf of bread and some honey in a tin. He puts them with the other lumps of our things under the tree, black against the glare.

Captain Sava glides into view on Sunday morning, standing in the bow of the boat coiling his rope, coming closer with a pounding sound.

A little crowd with similar faces and one black umbrella has gathered from different directions. A shepherd throws his three rams in the water with a whoop and frightens them out towards the boat. Agroti coasts me out in the loaded skiff, while Sava hoots orders from the wheelhouse, staying out of the sun.

Finally a swimming donkey scrambles aboard on a plank and a sheet of tin. Then we head out in a straight line, following a band of calm water that widens back like a roadway through the dark blue, leaving a tiny unfamiliar bay behind, the island melting above it, all wrong.

YANNI'S HOUSE

'YES ... YES.' PIETER, THE DANISH CONSUL FROM
Iraklion, draws on his pipe, and nods once with a glance at
me. He looks up at the green shoots standing tall on the
arbour, just starting to bend over the bamboo crosswork. He
blinks behind his smoked glasses and relaxes in his chair.
We're quiet again.

Two men with black headcloths ride by on the road,
shouting back and forth. Over them, between the trees, the
bad idea of Gavdos and the little, similar clouds beyond it
lie like stepping-stones away across the summer sea.

Here, however, there's only the consul in his white summer clothes, the tall consul talking to me, as sure as a giant,
with his ring of red hair around his head. I've never seen him
before. He got here too easily. I thought I was hidden. Was
my name on a list?

We sit with our arms folded, watching our shoes. I'm
solemn and dull with strangers. I just sit still until they've
gone. A *disaster*, I say to myself each time.

I carry the cups inside. I'm not going out again. Katina
has taken advantage of the inexplicable visit to slip inside and
go to sleep with her eyes rolled and her caked feet on my
pillow. From my window I can see the consul's blue car

pulled up in the turn of the road, as if it's fallen there from the sky.

'Oh, well – ' I remember he said to me in the courtyard with a young laugh skyward. I'd repeated something he'd said, and he just laughed and waved me away. His advice – that I should leave here – was the furthest thing from his mind now, you see. That was the way he spoke. He said something and then backed away from it. But he'd still made the point: you remembered he'd said it, and afterwards the day wasn't quite the same, because someone had come and doubted you. No, he only shrugged his head and made a clicking noise at Sofia, who watched him with one eye covered. 'Not that bad,' he said to me. 'Not so bad as that. Look, this is no official visit. I am like you, having a holiday of it, you know. That's all. I supposed you would be interested.'

'Why did you say Sicily?' I asked him, and he said,

'Oh, because it is west, I suppose. It's considerably nicer there, the entire situation.'

Who would believe this? I wondered if he was confusing only to me. I asked him if he wanted to crack some almonds, but he shook his head.

'Also, because I have been there in Sicily some time,' Pieter said. 'It's quite lovely, I think. Taormina. Many writers there. And, you know, far less trouble than this that we have on Kriti.'

I move in slow-motion with strangers, defensive, posing. I never hear a thing. And no one really cares, that's what is odd. For an hour or so, these big guests are merely surprised that I'm as tight as I am. Then they vanish, returning to somewhere they like better. It would never occur to them to settle out here in the trees. Each time, I think the next chance-visit will be easier. But it never is.

I can see the consul talking to Yanni. Yanni laughs falsely

and lights a cigarette. He scratches his forehead and shifts his hoe from hand to hand, seeming wild and small before the important man in white.

All night, my feeling of safety is gone. Maybe there's something I don't know about – something Pieter knows, maybe something everyone knows? I half-remember this same feeling of being gone around and left foremost, unaware, in the real state of things, as if it's happened somewhere before, a long time ago.

'Yakovo sees clouds,' Yorgi says in the kafenion so I can hear. 'What are you writing, Yakovo? Eh? Tell us. There's something starting to go wrong, isn't there?'

Pieter's things aren't my things. I can't be caught in his hard world, not finally. But Yorgi can, and Kristo can, people I like and see every day.

'Do you know what will happen?' Yorgi says. He sits down backwards on a chair. 'Listen a minute: I'll tell you. A war, Yakovo, devil take it! A war like '48. First a little one, to move things a bit, understand? Then comes the big one!'

'Nothing, nothing,' says Kristo, pulling down his mouth, tapping his lighter around on the table. 'Bah,' he says to me.

'Quiet, now,' gurgles old Barba Hajimikalis, leaning on his stick. 'Not just a war. Things wider than wars.'

'A war, though, Yakovo!' Yorgi says. 'Saints-big! Brothers biting brothers, fields finished, houses burned, everything down again!'

I haven't been watching these hot summer days that leaf by one by one. Now I wonder if they're simply running out. Should I go or stay? If you have to go once, then don't you always have to? Does it even matter so much what happens to me here? I can't seem to think about things, things explode when I consider them.

Everything seems like a warning, even little things I see when I ride along the road. But soon, once again, I'm convinced that my situation depends only on me and on what I've brought around me. I write in my notebook that *I'm the guide of this*. It just comes back to the grove and the house and this table by the window. Morris depends on me. He noses his empty sack of carob beans by the gate and calls with his tail out straight.

Yet Pieter said, 'It is here that you may soon lose this guiding that you keep talking about. *When in fact you are quite out of touch.*'

It's true. I have only the details of the place to tell me things. Sometimes I think my life began here, and that it will always be too early to go. The past is still too close, the past is still the lemon grove, the past is the road. I won't be hurried.

Sometimes while the bucket is filling at the spring, I look down the coast of light and dark blue ridges to the east, and I try to imagine another time in another place. But it would take more possibilities than I have to leave here right now. Possibilities from the day-moon, possibilities from the sea.

The centreless story of these days is just a record of what happens when I'm writing. No one comes around, the day gets later and later. Maybe it takes someone like Pieter to make a hub for things. I'm working all the time, but it feels like I'm writing on days, not on pages of paper, and ruining them.

Espasia makes up excuses to come in and see what I'm doing, always sitting in the same place. She gathers the dry clothes off the bushes or picks an apronful of broad beans and comes backing huge and black in the door, always surprised to find me here at the table again.

Once, I called her over to see my work, because so few

others seemed as interested as she was. She took up the note-books and turned them sideways, looking at them with her empty blue eyes. She whispered, 'Write, Yakovo.' She touched the typewriter keys and said it was a marvellous machine, which it is, in fact. Now it's no longer a daily occur-rence, the rattle of the latch, her gifts and her startled face. It only comes in fits. Mostly, she passes my window with her face turned completely away. She comes each day and leaves something on the kitchen table – a few eggs, some olives or a plate of hairy yoghurt – to show she's been here, but that no one has heard her and no one has seen.

Yanni's Maria pays no more attention to me these morn-ings than Nikolo the new bee does. One would think she might want to look in now and then, but evidently not. I explain what I'm doing whenever I see her humping along the fence outside, and she makes little grunts of mild interest. But to her, Yanni just hunts, Yakovo just writes, Maria just works –

So I'm usually left alone with my endless trains of thoughts in the corner of the room, with my cup of pencils and Sofia. I open the bottom half of the door at noon and have a rest and a cigarette, watching everything go by around me. Sometimes it feels as though nothing holds still long enough for me to see it. Nothing recurs.

All the things I need are here: I even live in a certain kind of magnificence. Yet if I'm to stay here longer, I see I must build something solid and new to hold it all together in the ugly face of things. Maybe a small, small house: a writing house under the glossy carobs by the road, just one room with a sea-window.

Yanni will help. He hangs his gun and his greatcoat on a branch, jams half a cigarette in his cigarette holder and looks

over the ground with me. It's not a strange idea to him: he
draws a big square in the grass with his boot heel. The rest
of the day we fight rocks down the hill to break up with
a sledge-hammer. In the twilight he's still cutting trenches
where the thick walls will go. I pay him fifty drachmas.

In the morning, Maria arrives in her unravelling grey
sweater and a borrowed skirt, bringing me almonds and
anthótiro cheese in a sack. Before God, she doesn't have time
for this, but Yanni's told her to come out here and clean my
kitchen. Move now, so she can work. And her Mikalis climbs
up on the roof from the fig tree and begins to gratuitously
patch the holes with some clay he's brought from the river,
calling bored good mornings to everyone who rides by.

Then comes Yanni himself, the captain of it all, just awake,
wanting coffee. While we're digging a pit to keep the shell-
lime in, I tell him that after this initial period of heavy work
I will go on with the house myself, since I don't have much
money this month. But he says money doesn't matter – leave
the money! Only, because I might not be here forever – we
might put a plaque over the door that says *This is Yanni's
House.* All day he jokes about it, *Yanni's Work: Yanni's House.*
A plaque like the one on the canyon bridge.

'One day, I'll live here, I!' Yanni shouts to the little field
policeman, who stops on the road to watch us in his old
militia uniform and his peaked cap with a badge.

Each morning, long before the voices come out along the
road, I notice that Maria has brought her field a little closer
to the tussocky grass where the door of my new hut will be.

Her shaftless rake, her blunt pick and her helmetful of
seeds are lying in the trampled stubble well within the wall
trenches.

'They're hers – and his!' Manoli says in disbelief, kneeling to look closely at a hammerhead and a cracked axe. 'Not mine.'

There's no doubt about Yanni's self-interest in the building. But there is something more too. I see it when he puts his hands in his pockets and stands off at a distance, planning the day's work. 'More rocks!' he barks at me, or, 'Bring Mikalis.' His own half-whitewashed house at the end of the peninsula is a motley of unfinished projects – the skeletons of a boat and a new oven by the door, the cement path across the dirt floor, the topless wooden kitchen he began last year when a load of lumber washed into the lighthouse cove.

Now slowly, carefully, with the new ability to complete something, Yanni brings the walls up to the level of the blowing grass, tapping off the edges of the rocks with the axe, and fitting them into the bed of mortar and scree. The lines are perfect, even the gap he's leaving for the front door. He pulls up the marker-stakes with a flourish, rolls them around with my guide-string and tosses the bundle into his knapsack. When the four corners stick up like jaw-teeth, he tells me we need a trowel. We can't go on like this.

'Bad,' I agree.

'Ey, only difficult,' he says, cleaning my spatula on a bush. I've never seen him so serious.

'What else do you think we'll need to do the work well?'

'Nothing else. Only that,' he says deeply. 'You can afford it.'

So we load rocks for three days more, until Kristo brings back a shiny new Swiss trowel from Chania for eighty drachmas.

Walking out to the spring, coming back on the road, or writing up here in the shade of the boulders, I like to see the little house rising up by itself, darker near the top where the mortar is still drying. I like to see the large and small rocks frozen sideways in a conglomerate, always even and straight in the frames of white mortar. I can already make out the opening for the little back window that will look down the coast.

I spend more and more time around the site, building up the wall myself and bringing sand and burned shell-lime back from the beach with Morris. I fit in the three window frames Mikalis took from the mill. My new house is a centre for me. I can scarcely keep my eyes off it.

Just as often, I see Yanni working out there by himself with his things hanging on the carob branches and the smoke from the beach-fire curling over the fields again. He taps the stones in the quiet mornings, lifting them into place, squinting, stepping backwards to judge. But if I walk out there too, he starts to laugh and talk loudly, uncertain about me and him and the climbing house. He puts his shoulder against the walls to show how strong they've dried. He shakes my hand and shouts that tomorrow or the next day he'll bring Priest Steliano to sing his *Hosanas* so the roof won't fall.

Each new strip of wall remains hollow until the outer stones have set, balanced inward on sort of a trough. Yanni chinks the holes between them with smaller rocks and trowels full of mortar. Then he stands on a kitchen chair and starts filling the space inside, bringing it slowly up to a solid new level around the window slots.

Today Yanni's working in front, leaving the doorway empty right up to the roofline. There seems to be no real top to the door. He goes and sits under the plane tree, has a drink and thinks what to do.

'The roof won't hold over there, over the doorway, over the hole,' he says, pulling at his earful of white hair.

'It needs something across.'

'That's it, it's got to catch on a place,' he says deeply.

He walks back with the pick and knocks away a rough oblong from the wall-top on either side of the doorway. He comes inside where I am, measuring with a notched stick. Then he does the same thing for each of the windows, even the little back one which has stayed a narrow slit about five feet tall.

Yanni doesn't come back for two days, having solved this problem in some way I don't understand yet. Then on the third day, a Sunday, he spends an hour out here adzing an olive trunk to fit over the door. By arrangement, Mikalis and the field policeman come around to help roll the monster piece end over end up onto the wall-notches on two propped carob branches. An ammunition box fits snugly over the little back window, and a post from Manoli's field works fine over the window facing the road. I build in the sections of wall above, and then our house looks finished.

It begins to rain. An early rain falls all day and night, and the plaster darkens and runs in slow grey streams, sealing the walls solid. The corners go round and the little house sags in the centre. Mulberry leaves pile up in banks at the bottoms of the walls. Pale grass spreads over the edges of the mortar pit and erases the path we've worn to the spring.

Yanni appears once or twice more in the gloom to make windowsills, but he says the roof will have to wait for better weather. Then he disappears completely.

'Do I know where he is?' says Maria, as she drives a stake into the front wall of my house for her munching, scratching goat. 'Look at the squash all over the road, now ... all by myself here, and *yi* the beans have washed away, the devils. Early autumn! Are three cabbages enough to eat?'

I have no idea why Yanni doesn't come back. Maybe I pushed him out somehow by working on my house myself. My work should have been here at my table.

A week passes, then two, then a month. The clouds start to come seriously. I've probably rushed Yanni too much. 'Slowly-slowly,' he'd say dangerously, heaving another stone up on the wall.

'Yes, slowly-slowly, and I'll be writing here in the rain,' I'd say.

'No, you won't. Captain Yakovo won't sit in the rain.'

You don't want to be with Yanni too long. It's only a matter of time until he turns on you. Then you're simply not there for him, neither is your roofless house in the showers.

Just as Espasia can show you a different face, as suddenly as a shadow passes over the town on the peninsula. One morning she doesn't stop by the house. Nor the next morning, and the rooms and the view over the field become uncomfortable. The path along the fence is the shortest way to everywhere, but for two weeks I'll see her circling through the trees, observing the windows. And when I ride past her gate in the afternoon, she waits just inside the kitchen until I've gone by, peeping out at the wrong time. Why? You never know. Maybe a dog has been barking at death roaming in the town at night. Maybe my gifts haven't been as many or as good as hers.

When it's Yanni's turn to change, he whistles and repeats what you say, making a murderous-sounding question out of it. It's as though there were two Yannis and today you have the wrong one.

Or else he goes away, disappears like this. It's a flattening thing to do, going away from someone in this cramped place. Here on the plain's edge, it's easy to think maybe there's bigger trouble somewhere, like the back of something Pieter the consul meant. You think you see it in the trees, and the clouds say it too.

One day in September when the olives are knocking against the windows, I see a long beam stuck in the eye of the little house, slanting down into Yanni's field. There are no other signs of work around the walls, which have drooped steeply to the right and left, forming a crown over the door.

'Yakovo!' Mikalis comes and waves a rod of dead sparrows over his head. 'Yakovo, come!'

'Captain Yakovo! Come and eat!' Yanni calls over his shoulder, crouched over a smokeless fire he's made in a corner out of the wind. 'Did you see the beam? Sava brought it. Thirteen *ponti* across. Thirteen *ponti* of cedar. You have a roof.'

Mikalis takes off his enormous shoe and holds it against the rings of red wood, watching me and grinning.

'Very strong,' Yanni says. 'Now, the little poles – the ones we used to lift up the doorframe, remember? – ey, now we just put them across this big one. . . .' Yanni breaks off another cigarette and stands outside looking up with his hands on his hips.

'Easy!' Mikalis says through his nose. 'And there's your roof! And later comes the bamboo, Baba says. Then a little cement on top – *ok!*'

'Only now I see it,' Yanni calls in. 'It takes the beam to hold it all; I'll tell you, Yakovo, before, I didn't know how to do it. Ey, we go off for a bit, we think it over. . . . Right, Yakovo? We're the same, you and I, you skinflint, you liar!'

'So never mind,' Mikalis says agreeably.

And the work begins again. After their meal, we lay the wood across the wall-tops. Very pretty from inside. Yanni looks at them for a long time, then he tells Mikalis to make

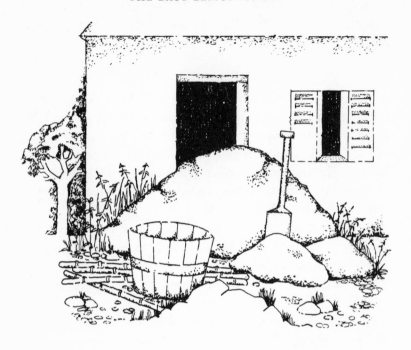

a ladder. For another week we build the walls higher, up and around the new beams, sort of closing them in.

Then Stelio, the cement mixer, comes completely drunk in his torn rubber boots, shouting directions before he even has his coat off. He jumps on the spade with both feet to loosen the cement bags Mikalis left out in the rain. I strip the knots and paper-bark off the bamboo with the back of a saw and pass each piece up to Yanni.

P. Arkilaki comes and asks what kind of metal-work we plan to use.

Yanni keeps licking his fingers and separating pieces of my writing paper, spreading them over the bamboo so the cement won't run down through. I go on helping Stelio. Mikalis goes off for water.

'Bed springs,' Arkilaki persists, 'iron fence posts, barbed wire – do I know what else? – spikes, tins, an axle. Only they've all got to be touching before the cement goes on,' he says, locking his fingers to show us.

'What stuff?' Yanni finally snaps, pausing.

'You don't want cement up there,' Manoli calls from the grove, and there's a silence. It's the first time he has come around while the work is going on. 'You don't want cement for that gypsy-house!' he says.

'Certainly not,' agrees meddling P. Arkilaki.

'Then?' Yanni shakes his head once, sitting motionless on the main beam with his feet hanging down.

'The house wants clay,' says Manoli.

'It wants a grenade,' P. Arkilaki says.

'Cement!' roars Stelio, standing still.

Manoli clears his throat and walks into the conversation with his mud-spattered knee-boots. 'Not cement, I say. Because the top of the house slopes this way and that. And because, of course, not even bamboo is flat.'

'And?' says Yanni.

'Ey, and. The cement will crack, maybe fall. Maybe Yakovo inside.'

Yanni spreads on another sheet of paper, then stops again to listen. Everyone is quiet.

'How much cement will you make, there above?' Manoli asks louder.

Stelio says, 'Going to be twenty *ponti!* Maybe more!'

'Twenty? Ah. About a ton, that is. On bamboo.'

'Not half that,' says Yanni.

'Even the half, even the half. And this one,' Manoli points to P. Arkilaki, 'This one knows: if you're going to have cement, you've got to have the iron inside it.'

Manoli likes clay roofs. Even if it's for a shed or a back-house, clay is always best because it doesn't leak. Not if you take a little time with it once a year. Naturally, if you don't take the time –

'What do we do now?' Yanni almost laughs. 'The cement's here. Stelio's ready –'

'I carried three bags of cement out here,' Mikalis says.

But Manoli isn't listening. He draws four shaky lines through the spirals of figures and diagrams already on the back of his cigarette box. 'First, you spread on five *ponti* cement. You see? That little doesn't need iron. Then two *ponti* more, without pebbles. Build a siding around it. Then put on a clay roof.'

'Where's the clay?' asks Yanni.

'By the river,' quacks Mikalis.

'I have clay,' Manoli says calmly.

'What kind of clay, for instance?' Stelio wants to know.

'Ey, clay. What should I tell you? Red clay, yellow clay. One day, I'll show Yakovo.'

'Bring the bucket!' Yanni bellows at Mikalis, who goes off to the house at a dead run, only his legs moving. Stelio sets his teeth and slashes into his work.

'*Ba-baa!*' Mikalis hunkers down by the fence to look at us under the trees. 'Espasia won't give the bucket. It's for the drinking water, she says. And she wants Yakovo to bring the chair back.'

So the four of us hold a bread tub up against the wall while Yanni empties it time after time with the Swiss trowel and his hand. An hour later, a flimsy first-roof is done. Yanni scribbles his name in the fresh cement with a twig, just *Yanni's*. It's very sad. That's all his plaque will be. Everyone goes off crossly in different directions.

Manoli's lode of clay is as secret as Kristo's cache of rifles and dynamite out here in the haystack.

He walks ahead of me over the islands of grass in the flooded grove, whacking the heads off thistles, stopping now and then to see if we're still alone. He moves on under the branches and works his way over the walls, swinging up his legs, holding his hoe over his head. The withered lemons drop at the slightest brush, startling up the little clouds of flies sleeping in them. Manoli pauses again and again to listen or look in a tree, or close a water ditch to a hidden plot of okra. And Morris shuffles along alone up on the road with his empty panniers swinging, stopping when we stop.

Finally we come to a cut in the slope by the canyon chapel, so close under it that the pointed graves and the little blue cupola are covered in the tall grass. Manoli kneels and pulls aside a mat of heather with his hoe. He pins it back with a stone so I can see the rich tan and red sides of his family's clay pit.

'Yakovo, take what you need. But don't go back by Arkilaki's path,' he tells me. 'Bring the donkey down the beach instead. People talk.'

I unload the panniers in the moving shadows of the carobs and throw the neat-cut blocks of clay up on the roof one at a time. I put them in rows and tramp them flat. Manoli comes up the ladder and approves. He shows me how the winter washes things together. It seems hopeless at first, but time and again I start down between the lanes of shoulder-high walls, turning towards the cypresses by the church, then back along the coast through the winding, tarry driftwood. I watch the lazy sleeping shells and the little dark-eyed soles skimming along close by my feet. The sea washes tirelessly in spreading its hazy, fleeting colours on the surface until they slowly fade away one by one.

At the end of the week, I carry out a straw mat, my folder

of work, a table and a chair. It's really a very nice house. Pieter should see it.

There will be a feast for the workers tonight. I spread one of my long striped sheets on the table and light three candles in a line. I've plastered my hair down with water and put on a clean blue shirt.

Espasia comes first with a ball of brown dough and a bag of cheese mixed with mint. She goes about quietly in the church-light of the glowing candles – to the skillet, to the oil bottle, to the water bucket with her long skirt sweeping back and forth across the floor.

Maria arrives with a necklace of orange beads, carrying a load of carrots and her black patent leather shoes rolled in a newspaper. She puts a whole cauldron of my oil on the fire and drops a little fish in from her cupped hands.

'And Manoli wanted to give fish too,' Espasia says, having brought none herself. She builds another fire outside on the stone bench to cook the celery and carrots. 'And beans, he wanted to give, lentils, beef –' The frying smoke fills the courtyard and trails out over the south field across the road to the water.

'Quick!' Maria shrieks inside. 'Oh! Oh!' Katina bolts out the door with her mouth full and her tail between her legs, and a corrugated hand throws a hammer after her.

Yanni and Mikalis stalk along the fence carrying window glass, too busy even to look through. Stelio weaves after them, steadying himself on the oven ledge with a huge knife in his belt.

Finally, Manoli totters up on the road bank in his black clothes. He waves a finger – he'll have a word with me. He comes walking slowly in towards his old house, straight across the empty field.

THE WINTER FIELD

I STOPPED UNDER THE FORTRESS WALL TO READ THE instructions for Mourner Tasoula's new steam iron.

O. Carter Hicks, Ltd, Birmingham (some insanity of wheels and cranks, some darkness of power wires and smoke stacks, some scribble of ugliness up there):

> *being watchful of the water displacement aperture. For petticoats, set the Wessex Timer at 4A flow, 3A for silk trusslets . . .*

Whatever that means. I can never see the goods for the places they come from. Yet I'm becoming a figurehead for the steadily mounting modernities in Paleochora, almost an agent. Birminghami, Stuttagarti, Pittsaburgi – I know how to work things from all those places. Last week, I showed Mikalis how to shoot a fish gun from Marseilles.

Pappa Steliano was digging below me in the little oblong platform of his garden, working alone high over the town with his cassock tucked in his waist-cord and his long black hair waving over his shoulders. I wondered how he would bring these two merging worlds together. Would it happen slowly while he was digging?

The track to Tasoula's hut curled through the crumbling

russet mound of the fortress, then it dropped between the last poor houses towards the winter pier. The electric line followed lazily down over the red rocks to touch a few of the overlapping roofs, and then it lifted and turned away to the lighthouse. Shadows flitted along ahead of me down the airless corridors. The gravel crunched invisibly on the other side of the walls, keeping up with me, but there were only the sounds of scratching hens and coughing.

Mourner Tasoula shook talcum on my wrists and gave me a stool by her sunflowers. She talked about the sadness of her Easter work, and she gave me a tinselled chocolate that fell to powder in my hand. Then she handed me the steam iron. I'd kept the instructions for two weeks. Four other women came in too and stood in a circle while I felt down the machine's grey-and-black striped cord and touched its sleek, spotless nose. Tasoula held the paper for me to read as I worked.

'*Yi, nahto!*' A nail-less thumb reached from behind me and pushed up a barely visible latch on the handle with a click.

'Yes, that's for the water,' I said. 'The water must not go below – here. That's what most of the writing is about.'

'Ah-h? Not below there?'

'No.'

'Here, for instance, not?'

'No, it will burn your *flanélla*, that way,' I said.

'That's all? It's that easy?'

'Nothing else. Only you've got to know once,' I said.

'What can I give him, what?' Tasoula groaned, looking around her solid stone yard with her Birmingham iron in her hand. She went inside her hut and lifted the flowered cloths nailed to her shelves. She scanned the walls filled with lit ikons and coloured pictures of Christ. Then she went out the back door and up the hill to a niche in the rocks where a little whirlwind of feathers and onion peels was blowing.

'Really, I want nothing!' I called.

'Sit,' the others said.

'I didn't even look at the iron paper until today.'

'Wait,' they said. 'Sit.'

'There!' Tasoula came back with a thick bundle of cabbage and lettuce seedlings, another chocolate and a ball of seed potatoes tied in a new apron.

'Well, many thanks,' I said.

'Nothing!' Mourner Tasoula laughed and crossed herself. 'Good weather! Good rooting! It's rich work, a field. Hm! It's not bad work!'

I just said yes.

The bundle of potatoes hung on a peg over the fireplace with my hat and the last plaited onions. The cabbage seedlings lay tied together on the window ledge outside with Yanni's work clothes and the rat's nest of other things Sofia carries up there to sleep on. After a while the white roots started reaching back into the corners of damp dust, trying to get under the window. Sometimes the oddest things beg not to be thrown away. Now Espasia has brought them in from the pouring rain today.

'When you leave things behind, it means you want to forget them,' she says, splashing into the kitchen.

'What will Manoli plant for the winter?' I ask her, warming my hands on my coffee cup, enjoying my fire. Sofia stretches and purrs under the streaming window.

'Ey, what, Yakovo? Manoli's sick,' she says with a look at the lettuces on the bookshelf. 'Yanni's planted and gone away ... Kristo's off in the taxi....'

The winter should be a time of rest and peace, or at least a time of holding one's own during the cold.

One ought to be inside. The saddle needs to be fixed, and there are tools to be sharpened and shafted and roof-leaks to be stuffed. A book could be written. A bath could be arranged. All you have to do is look outside to see it's a completely different time.

Of course, this is too fine a thought for Paleochora, where people are still joylessly fighting up windbreaks and falling in the mud. Here on the south coast, there's no let-up at all – the same crops always being planted, the same disasters rolling afterwards, the same people moving on the same paths around the house. There's no idea of alternation, whether of field soil or daily work. Just a constant, purgatorial trudging.

Up in the north, they like to let the climate set the pace of the year. They're gentle, seasonal people, and they think of things like that. They concentrate on oranges; they don't grow much else up there in the winter. The fields lie fallow until it's warmer, and then everyone comes out at once and ploughs the earth over rich, dark brown, finding plenty of worms and other evidence of the rhythm of things.

But not here. 'Oh, here you can keep your crops all year!' the women call proudly from the fields along the road.

No wonder the melancholy of the southern spring, and the curious irritability all year.

'Tear it down!' Elia the ploughman bellows at the house. He stops his yoked mule and ox in the downpour before the stick-gate. 'Too small! See? Can I get through here? No!'

So I'm in on it again from the very first, even the ploughing day. I stop writing and pull on my poncho.

It's different in the summer. It's clearly a time for balanced work in the sun. In the summer, I turn over the ground and hoe the furrows myself. I write in the morning and hoe in the afternoon. I hoe so slowly that the corn and the beans are up before I've planted the cucumbers. In fact, I grow melons in the shade of the corn, late into the season until they finally split open from the heat in the air. People always ask me for the seeds, and how I can grow fruit in August.

Now Elia turns his team dumbly around while I fix a chain on the taller gatepost to pull it down. 'It takes longer here, it takes longer,' he warns as the wood splinters, snaps and yanks free across the soaked grass with my scythe still stuck in it.

Espasia waits silently, confused, at the side of the field with her round baskets of onions and wrinkled seed potatoes. P. Arkilaki looks on from the roadbank in his blue gym shoes with white dots on the ankles. Greasy, economizing P. Arkilaki, who lets his tomato plants double as bean poles.

Elia puts the blade into cutting position, takes hold of the handles and lets the plough speed through the poppies, swerving on around the medlar tree in the middle with a yell and a whistle. And then Espasia and I begin moving along behind, dropping and covering the cut potatoes. By the time the team reaches the fence and turns around to come back again, a paring of rich scarlet has fallen neatly in a straight line, revealing the same sandy soil and grey sea-stones.

'Ap! Stee! Oriesteh!' The heavy feet start clomping stupidly again, and Elia follows with the reins, peering through his thick glasses as he trudges back over the first segmented cut.

Espasia and I break the clods and knock the soil off the old tomato stalks and throw them over to the sides. There are too many rocks and shards to bother about. It would seem that any kind of greenery might have been good for the ground, left to mulch and rot in the rain while one got his own bearings on the year. But no one's ever done that here. The speargrass stands as tall as a man along the fence, from the centuries of weeds tossed there from the lower, poorer level of the winter field.

'Plant the cabbage and lettuce today, Yakovo!' Espasia says happily behind me. 'I'll get them for you. Where are they? Inside with the books?'

'For sure!' says Elia, passing. 'And the potatoes! With

this little rain they'll grow like trees!' Friendly Elia gets seventy drachmas and half the potato crop for his morning's work.

'What else are we planting?' P. Arkilaki finally calls, stepping closer through the flowery threshingfloor. 'What are we planting today?' Espasia makes a face and signals me not to tell him. 'Probably some more foreign things again?' Arkilaki drones. 'That tall celery you don't have to cook? The round cucumbers again?'

'Little from each!' says Elia with a wink. 'Right, Yakovo? *Ad-eh! Stee!*'

The plough catches on a long white object. A peeled mulberry stick. We stand up to see it with our legs spread wide. Appears a bulb of stuffed sacking with a face made of coloured yarn. It's my bearded scarecrow from the summer. Elia mumbles something and tosses it away as hard as he can with a flutter of its red and white stocking cap. 'It's harder here at Yakovo's, more complicated, I say ... *kúkles*, now ... dollies, eh? ... who knows what else you find around here....'

'Oh, a lot of things you find in the ground here!' Arkilaki turns away from the fence and walks off. 'A lot of things,' he calls meanly. Espasia wipes her nose and crouches on again in her soaked black clothes, thinking of her dead son, Vasso, and the mine his plough hit, or maybe thinking of nothing at all.

'Never mind! One day – *stee-ah!*' Elia goes down in the mud with a curse and crawls after the reins, '... one day out west on the Kondoura ... working Prokopi's old place, and *dok!* the plough's caught, mule can't move it. What is it but a bomb from the Germans! Big, hoo! ... two oil drums together ... blow you over the Pelikano! Bigger than big! Well, stood there ... looked at the devil ... finally just left the plough for the gypsies.'

Elia makes one more pass down the centre of the field for the main water ditch, and then he runs the rib-furrows across it, about a yard apart. After that, he hooks his plough over the yoke and starts back to town with the loose chain ringing away along the road.

A little sun comes again, it dries the furrow tops and whitens the branch-propped fence. I throw out fans of carrot seeds, moving down along the roadbank, with two jeering black crows jumping along behind me. The last cicadas are calling brokenly in groups, and hearing them, I realize how much I have ceased to notice.

I plant the limp seedlings high on the furrow sides, so the standing water won't spoil them. Morris brings in two fat sacks of his manure. I tramp it into a paste and fill the furrows up flat. After a few days, most of the plants are standing up in the wind, and a mist of green onion shoots covers the long inset bed I made. But the plot of potatoes is unchanged, still weed-flecked and empty along the border of wide-open poppies.

The land, with its changes and limits, makes a difference in the long rolling clouds. The muttering thunderheads stop and tower high over the clearing, colossal head on head, budding straight up so I can barely see their tops.

It's warm today, and the sweet smell of gorse is coming down from the hills. Without the glaring summer sun, the eye traces out the exact lines of the canyon ridge, and the caves and cliff-weeds and hanging pines. I hang my shirt on the gate and look for the shine of the hoe in the grass. I walk down the bank of broad green leaves, reluctantly pleased at the bit of order I've made.

'The field's good!' Andreas the cobbler calls, rocking by, disappearing behind the trees for a moment. 'Late, though!'

'A little late,' I agree.

'Now: wheat! It's already the time for wheat!'

So one is to go from one job to the next, never feeling, never seeing much? That's how Andreas lives, anyway, in a kind of roving temper, always half-tired.

'Ah, Yakovo, Yakovo-o! Too late!'

I build the earth up around the notched cabbage stalks and cut off the yellow first-leaves that tip down, frayed, with the black butterflies flitting low around them, looking for places to stay.

I barely feel the weak sun on my shoulders and hands. But it's flowering the lettuces, just clusters of saffron florets blowing foolishly on thick, crooked stems. I cut some of them for Willy and hoe the gaps flat.

A plane comes rumbling and knocking around the west coast, making innocently out to sea. There's a silence, then a sparkle of its orange double-wings and a sudden rasp of power. It drives straight in over the trees on the plain with a trail of pink spray floating down even before the beach. Then not a sound, not a bee in the air.

Mercifully, more strong rain falls, drying just once in sickly copper-green smears around the lemon trees and my flooded writing house. Now it pours down more or less finally in dismal, endless sheets. Poisoned chickens and sheep lie by the roadside for Evangeli to cart away.

The bridge is out again. This time, it's turned on its side, seeming more hopeless than ever before, but leaving a narrow walkway. People go by the house on foot with saddle bags over their shoulders bulging full with potatoes and plumes of wild celery. And the north wind, in its usual way, begins to blow from every side at once, roaring down the canyon, coming in low over the stone walls in a solid, flat blast.

Espasia pins the tomato plants down while I hoe the rocky

soil up in hillocks around them so only the tops are showing. Only the beans seem safe, trapped on their sides under stone-weighted branches, flowering out of the wind.

The furrows are in a shambles, warped together, half blown away. I look back and think, 'The work was mine. Some of me is left there too.' Even as we move along, stronger winds are lifting the branches right behind us, teetering them up on end with a roar and cartwheeling them across the winter field, beans and all.

'It's not worth while! Let's stop!' I call. 'We'll lose the whole field today!'

'What? It's worth while, Yakovo! It's worth while!' Espasia finishes the row herself. She straightens and scowls at me, her black skirts flapping madly. 'What if you gave up? Where's your field then? What do you eat?'

'You eat things from the summer!' I say. 'Dried figs, almonds, you eat!' But in my mind I see heavy, bleached August again, the goats panting in the shadows, the plain reeling impossibly in the heat.

'What things, Yakovo? Eh? What's left? It's easy for you! You're going off somewhere! We have to stay!'

'Going off? Who?'

'Ey, I know, I know!'

Espasia pauses and turns her worried face up to me. 'Go inside, Yakovo! Never mind my onions!'

'Is this weather for a field? Let it go!'

'The wind will stop! Hm! That kind of a person!'

Katina starts barking at our voices. Willy's white face appears at the window.

We lift up one end of a fence section, wrestle it back to the side and drive in new stakes. There's a crash of something else behind the house. It's almost funny. Both of us stop and look that way. The arbour again? The beams of my hut?

'We haven't the weather!' I say. 'Look around!'
A rough sea today. Storm-birds. The waves on the horizon look like another shore with shining silver domes and towers.

In the warm halcyon the sky parts over canyons of red clouds and high streaks of blue. The hornets are humming over the field to the almond trees.

I cut five fist-sized cabbages and soak them in the water ditch by the gate where someone's tied a brown mule with a white ring around his eye. Yanni's Mikalis and a friend with a shaven head are talking drowsily and throwing their knives in the dirt under the mulberry tree. Kristo and Corporal Lazaro are down in P. Arkilaki's clover fields on the other side of the road. Manoli's alone, smoking on the bench in the courtyard with his hoe between his legs.

More and more each day, there is a vague, aimless motion around the house. Like a dream, only parts of the days seem clear to me, and the wholes of them are lost. People gather in groups, waiting in the shadow of the hill and under the murmuring lemon trees. They drift off slowly without plans – and reappear, the same ones in the same day, still without enough hope to begin something new.

Ploughman Elia sleep-walks by with a shotgun and a forage cap with ear-flaps. I ask him how his own fields are doing, and he smiles oddly and makes a flat sweep of his hand to say they're *finito*.

'Now what will you do?'

'Wait,' he says.

'Until spring?'

'Spring, spring,' he says, waking up a little and pushing away from the fence.

'Ey, *yasu*, Elia!' I start clearing the branches away from my healthy square of onions.

An hour later, he's nearby again, talking under the kitchen window to a shepherd with a shaggy cloak and field glasses around his neck, who drawls back, 'Well, it's about the same up there as it is here: hills of rocks, goats, and way down, a river –'

Espasia wanders in past me, closing the gate softly behind her. She stoops double and pulls up some long carrots.

'I may plant there again, they grew so well,' I say to her.

'Yes, Yakovo.' She smiles at the trees and the heathery hill as she walks away.

'Or better, maybe we'll put in some melons,' I say.

'Whatever you understand, Yakovo. It's your field.'

She's back again at midday to tie the sheep in the grove, looking glad with her bucket of chicken slops on her arm.

I lose track of who stops here and who passes on. The wrapped-up figures wander together on the road and group dully for the next season. It's the same down at P. Arkilaki's, and in the fields along the river.

Willy wonders at them too. He worms back and forth between their legs, following this one for awhile, coming back with another. He drops his head doubtfully each time, stops and jumps sideways, always finding himself alone.

The furrows in the field are laid open and covered with Elia's wide footprints. The cut cabbage stalks lean forwards and backwards in the waving wild grass, and the flowering let-tuces are tall orange-yellow fountains now, remarkable things, mockeries. Another month is finished, and only car-rots and onions are left of it. Morris eats the dry tangle of beans, closing his white teeth and stepping backwards, rip-ping yards at a time off the fence. I watch a partridge walk without a sound through the ruin of the winter field. When the wind stops, I feel an enormity of space beyond the clearing.

Points of speargrass are coming up through the broad yellow squash leaves. The hoe and the pick are lost somewhere in the daisy-covered confusion of fields, similar little worlds of many seasons, crossing wearily over one another, all gone. It seems too much to realize all at once, almost a secret, that no season is new.

I think of the fascination of the year's first rain falling, and the gales of crows sticking to the trees. I remember Maria's goat eating my carrots so calmly that I walked right by without seeing anything wrong.

Now the pickers are marching out along the road, stopping at the spring to fill their jugs. They disappear into the groves, then from all around comes the rattling of their sticks on the branches and the hail of the last yellow lemons dropping on the spread cloths.

Time passes, only Sundays come. Pappa Dimitri staggers down from his mountain service with his goat on a string. He stops under the plane tree and looks about him, tired and grey, as if he's just returned from another country where the people are different and the language is different.

Today, a group of loud Spanyakans with rifles come trotting down the road behind the carobs. The first of them glances at my cigarette smoke coming out of the shade, and he leans back to see me better, holding his reins up close to his chest. '*Yi*, the big foreigner!'

'Who was that?' Manoli calls from the east field, which he's hoeing back bare for his lentils. It's hardly the same place now, flat, dark at the end where the water is glittering across the path.

'Some kapitano on the road,' I say with a shrug. My voice sounds strange in my ears. Suddenly everything strikes me with the force of a memory. I look at the fig tree bent over the roof, at Sofia's black tail hanging down from the window, at my empty little plot inside the fence, and I can't believe this is what I've been doing.

'Eh? Who?' Manoli asks from his flooding field, where his squares of lentils will be sown under the same windbreaks of corn.

JOURNEYS

TWO GYPSIES LOOKING FOR WOOD CAME INTO THE
clearing towards the house, exactly as I would have
imagined. One of them strolled right across the winter field,
stepping over the piled tomato stakes and the fallen fence.
The other loped through the scrub at the side, cutting the
straight grey sprigs of wild lilac.

They slouched through the courtyard without a glance,
as if it were theirs, and the view in the window was left bare
and stricken, picked over in some last, new way.

They crossed the road and went in among the beach fields,
the first gypsy still hiking ahead on his long stilt legs, with
his cloth hat pulled down low and his brown hands jumping
at his sides, and the second one moving slower, missing nothing. They were going away again, so dark against the green,
like a visit from a far place, only for me to see.

'We want a little wood,' the nearest one, the cutter, said
softly when I followed them out as far as the plane tree.
'Yours? Yours?' He gestured around him to the grove and
the boulders on the hill, starting back towards me with his
black hair blowing. The first stood turned ahead without
moving.

'Manoli's,' I said.

'Manoli's.' He narrowed one eye and frowned and smiled at the same time. He looked past me to see if someone else was around. 'Where's Manoli?' he said.

'What is it Manoli there wants?' the other called in a whisper, coming back too.

They wore different layers of coloured shirts under their old coats full of holes. A fish-line of blue and green beads hung from the button on the cutter's sleeve, and he had an earring with a red stone in it.

'Where are you going?' I asked him, and he shifted his armload of wood to the other side.

'But the big house there is yours,' he said instead.

'Not even that!' I told him. 'Are you going far?'

'Where would we go? We're going right here,' the other answered meekly, stepping closer and tapping my chest too hard with the backs of his fingers. 'Here – and above to make baskets with your wood.'

They saw me, and yet they didn't see me. They heard me, but they weren't really here. Rootless, agile, with nothing to lose, they were living so close to life that they had its same vague force. They took all my thoughts away. From this day forth, I said to myself, I'm a traveller leaving on a journey.

'We'll walk around until we have what we want,' the cutter said plainly as he lit a cigar.

'Can you make a basket for me?' I asked.

'Maybe,' they said. 'Do you have the money? Curved basket? How long?'

'Wait. I'll show you.' I went back under the hill where Morris's tail was flicking in the speargrass. I heard the bundle of sticks drop in the weeds behind me. They didn't smile or speak after I left, but stood close together looking around them at the possibilities of the place.

The cutter came walking to me with one hand extended

to take the donkey's rope. He led him under the plane tree, and in one motion he made a slip-noose, deftly dropped it around a clump of heather and pulled it tight under his rubber-tyre shoe.

'A deep basket: one.' I showed them how I wanted the basket to hang from the side of the saddle. 'And with a hole in the bottom,' I said. 'A place, a *hole*, where I can rope the basket under his belly.'

So they sat on the ground with their backs against the cracked wall of my writing hut. The taller one did the weaving. He took up two pointed pieces of lilac, locked them in a cross between his long fingers and began to plait in strips of willow and green oleander from the other's load.

'Look,' he said, pausing and pointing sadly to the broken shoes he'd kicked off in the grass. I showed him my own torn boots, and he nodded and looked suspiciously at my hands.

He sat cross-legged, holding his work in front of him. He rimmed the basket bottom with dark, hard twigs. He passed it automatically to the cutter, who put his cigar on a stone and spun the woven piece around in his hands, pulling it tighter against his stomach and ticking off the ends with his knife. They moved surely and evenly, as if their point of interest lay just beyond the work and they didn't make mistakes of their own. Before, there was nothing but the sticks on the ground, and now a tan and brown basket was growing up from their hands in a gentle curve.

A piggish woman riding on the road laughed and turned on her palms in the saddle. '*Tsigáni!* What do they want with you, Yakovo, the *tsigáni?*'

The weaver gazed back calmly, his fine fingers moving low out of sight, the basket spinning and climbing on his outstretched legs and the knotted bamboo strips whipping in the air over his head.

Andreas came by next with his hands in his leather apron, but he never looked up from the road.

The gypsies finished an edgeless handle for the lid with a braid of white mulberry. Then they rolled the tall basket out under a tree and gripped my arm, talking to me with the strange emotion of people always driven out of everywhere on their endless journey. The cutter turned the basket over and stood on it, jumped on it once, watching. They touched their fingers to their foreheads, either thanks or goodbye, and turned and went back the way they came.

Espasia saw it all, circling deep in the dripping trees.

Now Yanni stands in the doorway with his thumbs in his belt, admiring the queer closed basket on the bed. 'Never mind, it's all right.' he says. 'Funny-looking, maybe a little wrong, eh? Eighty they took? Bah, for you, that's all right.'

He's brought Chennedy, his new hunting dog, precocious, ugly, evidently very low in the pecking-order of dogs.

He wants me to lend him a hundred drachmas. 'If you want to,' he says proudly, and Chennedy yaps proudly too.

'Don't worry,' he says quietly as we go outside. 'Tomorrow, Yakovo, you'll have it all back, I swear. Good person,' he says as he pulls out his wallet, only a fold of leather with a piece of wire to hold in the red and white bill. I'll always wonder where all that money went. It seems like Yanni has had to pay out more than anyone I've ever known.

'Tomorrow, or the next day,' I say. 'Sometime. Does it matter? Forget it.'

That was unusual. He pinches his cigarette stub between his fingers and throws me a glance, then he lifts it to the spring hornets bumbling along the wall-top, to the hollow dune of morning glories all along the front of the house. Yanni cuts

an apple in two for us, grins and looks at me for the last time, still puzzled.

Then naturally his Maria comes the next morning, to ask, too early, for the heavy things I'll have to leave behind. I'm making money-gifts these days, the best, most final kind of gifts, so of course I must be leaving. May my life be a happiness up there, and may we all live a hundred years.

I've already cleaned my room for the day, but Maria still wants to sweep while I work. She shakes the mats out the window and tells me to lift my feet. She jams *Emerson's Essays* back into the shelf upside down. She says she likes my spoiled goat and the bulky plates I can't take with me, all the firewood too, the useless field tools, and even the fragile lanterns.

Then Espasia comes and hears a rat in the gypsy-basket. I tell her it's the pencil I'm sharpening. But she carries Sofia over there asleep and lifts the lid, exclaiming twice, 'It's full!'

Espasia would rather have the kitchen table than all the little things Maria liked. She puts a handful of eggs on it and runs her fingertips over its meal-darkened top, tracing out the years of lettuce and macaroni caught between the boards. She says she'll miss me. She's brought a broad bean for Willy to eat, but he's outside somewhere.

Even Tasoula the Mourner, who seldom leaves the peninsula, calls a terrible *Good Day!* down from the spring. She moans in the news that the gypsies have come.

A ladder bumps against the side of the house and Manoli's little nailed boots climb up over the window a step at a time. My eyes follow his red-lipped water pail jerking up after him on a rope. Soon there are scraping, gnawing sounds above that frighten out a bright-eyed lizard and make Nikolo the bee grumble uneasily in the bamboo ceiling.

So I draw a line after my last word, *somewhere*, and walk around the side of the house. I climb onto the roof and crawl out past the melted chimney to where Manoli is sitting in the stubble with his tools.

'Good day, Yakovo! Are you still here?' he says. Manoli likes to sit almost on top of his work when he's mending a clay roof. He keeps his water, his fluff of wool and his manure bag between his spread boots.

'Pay attention. Once a year, just a few minutes up here, and you'll always have a warm winter,' he says, touching my arm lightly with his axe. 'Yakovo, there's no need to go.'

I see Espasia moving across the fields toward the piled stones of the sheep pen. Above it, over the trees, the Chania bus boils up a trail of dust, turning north towards the canyon mouth with a faint waver of music.

Manoli chops down until the roof-crack narrows to a line. The next one he finds goes all the way to the bamboo. He douses them with water, makes little balls of manure, wool and straw and presses them down with his thumbs. Then I carry his pail to another bad break over the door.

Manoli holds his axe with both hands, brings it shakily down to a foot or so over the hard clay and then digs and curses with his white hair flying up in flames. Not much of the old roof even shows anymore. Then he sits resting and buttoning his black sleeves, with the sagging roof mottled and patched everywhere behind him.

In Paleochora, the tiresome little sergeant leans back with a snigger, smoothing his clipped moustache with two fingers and looking from face to face. The field policeman makes

a long, disapproving spit into the sun on the street in front
of Yorgi's. A rat is running across the rooftops.

'Maybe a war, unless our Yakovo can do something,' the
sergeant says. He resettles his glossy beaked hat. 'What will
you do, Yakovo?'

He's bored and wants to bother me. He's forty-five or fifty.
He's from Lasithi, from the north, the usual round, northern
face you see from the bus.

The doctor from Vouta smiles politely and rolls his filter
cigarette under his shoe. He looks at his wristwatch and gets
up with his bag, starting on down the street to the next scrap
of blue cloth hung from a window.

'Ey, stop. Yakovo's a good *Kristiáno*,' Kristo says after a
while. He stretches and gives himself a shake.

'Ah, is he?' says the sergeant, twinkling with malice again.
'Bring him a tea!' These same, slow days aren't good for
anyone.

Yorgi stops still with his tray, as if to receive a fist-blow
instead of just another order for a coffee. Then he nods
silently and shuffles back behind the counter.

A goat crosses higher up the street where a little twist of
dust is dancing along under the church wall. The field policeman hums with his high voice and taps his stick on the concrete. 'What time will you go?' he asks the ticket-taker from
the bus.

'Five, boy.'

So the bus will coast down between the eucalyptus trees
and onto the canyon bridge with a bump, grinding up
through the rocks to Spanyako again. And after an hour, the
cloudy twin peninsulas and the straight line of the north shore
will start to show ahead between the mountains. The bus will
come honking to a stop in the same lonely fold of tundra,
and the ticket inspector will bound up on his feet from the
brush and swing aboard. Then the loud music will play while

everyone's sick, winding down the foothills into the white garrison town of Vukolies, and a completely different afternoon. When I leave here, it won't be by bus.

'*Kristiáno*,' the sergeant muses, catching his beads with a snatch.

Inside the kafenion, Pappa Steliano's voice drones on and on as he reads a letter with an orange and green stamp to a man from Rodovani, who's listening as stiff as a board, crumpling his hat in his hand.

Kristo and Corporal Lazaro pound their cards down harder and harder until Kristo turns sideways and just looks at the canyon again while the other brightly plays his hand to the end.

The Gavdos boat turns slowly at the end of the pier, stretching its reflection across the still water. From behind the houses I hear the seagulls and the dip and push of oars.

The field policeman hums with his head on his fist. Yorgi pinches half a dozen glasses together and takes them down to the water tap. The sergeant blows out a line of smoke like a question mark and flicks his ash, watching me steadily. 'What are you writing? What are you thinking, Mr Yakovo?'

I'm thinking this is just the end of all I know, and not the new time yet. I'm thinking of a boat from Sitia, or possibly Kali Limanes. But I've got to find places for Morris and Katina along the way. And Sofia too. No, Sofia stays here. Turkey, Burma, I'm thinking. But if I say so, you might not let me leave. Maybe I'll just tell you Rodovani.

'Thinking where you'll go, right?' he says, pointing to himself as a fly settles on his nose. 'And I. I'm thinking the same.'

'Yakovo ... is going home,' Kristo sighs. 'Amerika.' He drums his fingers on the table, staring at his old motorcycle with its red patch on the tyre.

'There's trouble in Amerika,' says the fat sergeant. 'Every kind of trouble there. Po! Every sort of crazy thing going on.'

Why should I answer you? I look at your chinless face and your bristly neck folding down from underneath your hat, and I see you'll never understand.

A gypsy chair mender makes a wide detour around the front of the kafenion, his strands of tied rushes bouncing around him like a skirt. He stays away from us. From his endless journey here, he knows what happens in bored, new towns with buses.

Then another dark figure, with a purple shirt, lurches into view between the buildings on the back street, stops, pulls his cap straight and starts walking backwards. The Gavdos Manuso advances with a finger pointed at him, and crazy Vassili follows them both with his hands in his coat.

The sergeant strides across the street and down the alley, skipping once and pulling his coat smooth under his pistol belt. Yorgi arches back to see.

Now there's a shout, and two other gypsies dart like cats along the side. Another one squatting under the post office wall decides it's time for him to run too. He ducks away with his basket, straightening and looking back from further down the street, as if nothing has happened.

'You stole five loaves of bread!' Manuso's still walking to-wards his same gypsy, with his arm held out to guide him better through the gathering crowd that moves along at both sides, jeering and stepping behind one another, framing the ugly scene and keeping it alive.

Behind them all, come two women in red and orange full skirts, wailing at the walls of boarded windows as Corporal Lazaro leads their plum-coloured horse with a tambourine tied on it. A pack of dark, quiet children come last with a light ringing and ticking of bracelets, clearing the picture again, leaving no trace of the cries and the quick movements jerking on ahead.

The crowd broadens around the rickety stairs of the bakery where the gypsy leans back and folds his arms, breathing hard. Morris steps around the corner of the building, out of the way, and his rope goes taut.

'Where did you stop last night?' barks the sergeant's voice. All you can see is his hat.

The gypsy holds his throat and says, 'Near the other village.'

'Take your hand away, I can't understand. What other village?'

'There above. By the river. By the road.'

'The mill, he means! There were ten or twenty of them up at the mill yesterday!'

'*Tsigani*,' mutters Yorgi, squeezing in beside me, still drying a glass. 'You don't want to bother them, certainly – '

Manuso bursts past with a stick and all the faces part, so that the gypsy's high box-shoulders are right in front of me. He lifts his hands nimbly, as though to free himself. But the clumsy blow falls across his arm, hard, with a thud.

A breath is caught and there's a silence like a broken spell.

Manuso throws the club up against the stairs with a clatter, and he stalks back down the corridor to the crooked bakery door.

'You see?' the sergeant says after a pause. 'That's the way of it! Clear out! You get us angry, and now, you see – '

The gypsy rubs the hurt place on his arm and looks calmly from face to face to remember who was here.

A green-shawled girl stands behind him with her back against an oil drum, fingering her necklace of brass beads. Her gaze meets mine, sightless, opaque. It passes to Yorgi, to Kristo, to Vassili. Only her hand is moving in the stillness, pulling the beads slowly down one by one from her braided black hair.

Going home, I can still hear the creaking of their carts. I see their tracks in the new loam spread on the road outside the cemetery. It's evening and the plain is quiet and empty.

I roll up my work with relief and tie it with a string. I wrap the bundle around with brown paper, tie it again and weigh it in my hand. Not much! A nameless kitten stands up on his hind legs and puts out a paw for my finger, making a little peaked shadow on the wall.

Espasia told me she wouldn't come today, but as I left I saw her dodging alongside me on one of Manoli's tracks through the trees. When I waved to her, she ran sobbing up on the road and threw her apron over her head.

Then the scraps of walls along the sides darted up for the gate to the last lemon grove, just a flat stone crossing above to show it was a separate place.

Morris stumbled under the load as soon as we started to climb. All along the way today I've taken my things from the basket and left them on the tops of walls and in the crooks of olive trees.

Sofia never knew I left. She was still asleep in the bulge of the screen door, swinging out and back with a tinkle of the bell. Willy stood calling testily in the kitchen with Maria's rope around his neck, leading out to a fence post.

Katina's worried, she stays close to me today.

The road ends in the middle of a hill by a shrine with a trough and a pink almond tree.

From here the path goes down to a long village of brown

and white houses, either Epanochori or Agia Irini. Beyond it, the track narrows and winds across the tundra, climbing straight up out of sight under the white noonday clouds to the east.

Two Mazans have ridden up here to the spring and are wiping their boots with leaves and splashing water on their faces and hair, talking happily at the tops of their voices. One describes a pyramid with his hands, building up and up, while the other whistles and wags his head. This is where the journey starts for them. Here is the real life, at the shrine halfway where the road begins.

They pass me proudly, sensitively, with only a word and a wave of a finger. Even their mules barely notice me waiting under the tree out of the way. We seem to meet at our furthest points here and are glad to get around one another.